MOUNTAIN

OF THE

LION

The Great

Revival in

Sierra Leone,

West Africa

MOUNTAIN

OF THE

LION

The Great

Revival in

Sierra Leone,

West Africa

Donald Hugh O'Keefe

Mountain of the Lion
The Great Revival in Sierra Leone, West Africa

by Donald Hugh O'Keefe

©1996, Word Aflame Press
  Hazelwood, MO 63042-2299

Cover design by Paul Povolni

All Scripture quotations in this book are from the King James Version of the Bible unless otherwise identified.

Printed in United States of America.

Printed by

Library of Congress Cataloging-in-Publication Data

O'Keefe, Donald Hugh
    Mountain of the lion: the great revival in Sierra Leone, West Africa/Donald Hugh O'Keefe.
    p.   cm.
    ISBN 1-56722-192-0
    1. Revivals—Sierra Leone—History—20th century. 2. United Pentecostal Church—Missions—Sierra Leone. 3. Oneness Pentecostal churches—Sierra Leone—History. 4. Sierra Leone—Church history—20th century. 5. O'Keefe, Donald Hugh. I. Title.
BV3777.S530553   1996
266'.994'09664—dc20   96-20617
                                                                              CIP

To my wife, Abbie,
because she deserves this and far, far more
for the twenty-one years
she has given to follow me in my calling
as a foreign missionary.

ONE

I HAD EXPECTED West Africa to be primitive and undeveloped, and yet, looking down at Liberia from the commercial jet, I was stunned by the jungle with its rough dirt roads connecting distant villages. The villages were a scattering of brown mud huts with grassy roofs in compounds barren of any vegetation.

As a boy I had seen pictures just like the scene below me, but this was real. It wasn't some far-off exotic land to dream about. It was here and now. Suddenly, the romance of Africa was replaced with the sobering thought that my family and I were going to live here. This wasn't a camping trip where we would briefly rough it in the great outdoors, nor was it a two-week vacation where we would see the highlights prepared for tourists and then run back to our comfortable California home. We were going to live here.

When the plane touched down at Robert's Field we were excited, but dog tired from the all-night flight. When we walked into the sunshine we met another reality of West Africa: the humid equatorial climate that surrounded us was like a sauna. We were soon sweating through our clothes and wishing we had worn lighter garments.

Over by the airport buildings we saw our welcoming party waving and yelling greetings to us. We were really glad to see them.

Of course, we had to go through customs and immigration procedures. Going through customs in West Africa is an unforgettable experience. Books could be written about the things that happen to people going through customs. No inexperienced person should attempt it on his own. One time a missionary's wife had a customs agent take her undergarments out of her suitcase and hold them up for public display while he and other agents laughed and made silly comments about them. She was red faced, but bravely ignored their game. There was no malice in this act—it was just the way West African customs operates.

Some things that happen in customs are not so harmless. If you do not know the ropes, or if nobody meeting you knows the ropes, you can go through some very unpleasant harassment and efforts to relieve you of your money or your goods. Thankfully, we were met by the Liberian missionaries, and with their assistance we survived customs.

The trip from the airport to the missionary's home was forty to fifty miles. Along the way it became evident that this land not only looked different from the air, it was different.

Women walked down the road topless, and men took baths in public completely naked. Teenage girls with their bodies painted white walked single file down the road as they participated in the initiation rites of the Bundo Society, a women's society based upon devil worship.

In some areas the road was lined with kiosks selling a wide variety of goods: used clothing, rice, palm oil, used motor oil, devil charms, and artifacts. The markets swarmed with people haggling over prices. The noise, the color, and the ripe smell of the markets are a part of the culture that everyone should experience—at least once.

The little add-on air conditioner in the Peugeot struggled to keep the passengers in the front seat cool, but it did little for those in the back seat. The dirt road we now traveled was not only rough, bouncy and winding, but, in addition, it had to be the dustiest road I had ever seen in my life. The dust rose with each passing vehicle to the height of a two-story building. Opening a window was completely out of the question. To see where we were going, sometimes we would have to stop until the dust raised by some passing vehicle settled. It seemed strange that such a dusty road would be lined on both sides with some of the thickest jungle in the world.

Finally, we reached the house, located in a little settlement called Brewaville. There we met a number of the Liberian church members who had come to welcome us. The people of West Africa are, for the most part, very friendly and hospitable. They are pleased to have visitors and they love missionaries for the message that they have brought and for the social and educational benefits derived from their labors.

It was good to be in a house surrounded by things familiar to us as Americans. Even though the electricity was off as much as it was on, and even though the well was going dry, we were glad to be there.

The dry well did cause some difficulties. We learned to take a bath with a single teapot full of water, for both lather and rinse. Sometimes we would go to a nearby river to bathe and wash clothes.

We had only been in Brewaville a few days when we had our first experience with driver ants. It was late at night and we were in bed when we heard a loud shouting outside. All of us flew out of bed and into our clothes. The missionary shouted to us, "The driver ants have come!" We didn't know what driver ants were. We had seen ants before, so what was the big deal?

But we had never, never seen ants like these. They came by the millions. It was an organized military attack by an army of voracious, carnivorous beasts intent on devouring everything in their path. Their black bodies were about a half inch long and very hard. They were vicious and aggressive. I found to my distress that these meat-eating mini monsters can bite like bulldogs and hang on just as tenaciously. If you pull them loose from your skin, a little piece of skin goes with them in their jaws.

In the darkness of the night I looked for the advancing horde that had already invaded the penned-in area where chickens, rabbits, goats, and pigs were kept. The Liberians frantically spread kerosene across the path of the ants and set fires in order to divert their migration away from the house and the farm animals.

This battle continued for hours. As I watched the war from what I thought to be a safe vantage point, I suddenly experienced a series of stinging bites on my legs. I looked down, and I was standing right in the ants. They had begun crawling up my legs, intent on consuming me.

I commenced a dance that was not in the Holy Ghost. I performed steps that were new to me and for which I had received no formal training. I realized that it was time to flee the scene. I made a dash for the privacy of our assigned bedroom where I could get my pants off and pick the black bulldogs off me. After I dispatched my assailants and got my trousers back in place, I went back outside to see how this epic battle was going. This time I was more careful in choosing a secure observation point.

After several hours of serious effort, the ants were diverted to other targets. None of the livestock was lost, and the ants did not get into the house. They could be a serious threat to life if a person was unable to escape them. Finally, we crawled back into bed in the wee hours of the morning.

The next several days were calmer, and we spent our time getting oriented to our surroundings.

As one of the Liberians spoke to the missionary, I asked someone what language he was speaking. I felt shocked and embarrassed when I was told that it was English. Later, when my ears became accustomed to Liberian speech I could discern that it really was English. The people have a singsong manner of talking that, when combined with their national accent and their habit of dropping all final consonants, makes their English incomprehensible to the uninitiated American ear.

The next weeks were a blur of activity: mission school closings, preaching assignments, meeting national preachers, attending rallies, learning administrative procedures, and so on. It seemed that people received the Holy Ghost in every evangelistic service. It was common to be in services where the church was literally overflowing. People had to stand around outside because they could not get inside. And the inside would be so tightly packed that people were actually like the proverbial sardines in a can.

Our first church service in Africa took place on a Sunday morning at the headquarters church in the capital city of Monrovia in an area called Sincor. The air was hot and oppressive that day, and inside the church, which was filled to capacity, the heat was even worse. My wife passed out during the service and had to be taken to the nearby home of Brother and Sister Albert Stewart to recover.

Brother Stewart was an army sergeant posted to the United States Embassy in Liberia who had come to the Lord while there. After a while he became the pastor of the headquarters church. He and his good wife were very kind to us. Later he and his family received full appointment as United Pentecostal missionaries to Liberia.

As we became better acclimated, we were able to cope better with the heat.

At the headquarters church my youngest son, Don, received the Holy Ghost and was baptized in the wonderful name of Jesus Christ. It was beautiful to watch my ten-year-old boy come out of the water with his hands in the air praising God in an unknown tongue.

During our months in Liberia, my oldest son, Mark, was used wonderfully of the Lord. Right from the beginning he took a liking to the African people, and they equally loved him. He seemed ready to adjust to the culture, and he endeavored to be used of God for revival. At this time, he was sixteen years old and had been preaching since he was fourteen. The resident missionary began to take him night after night to preach revival services. Always people received the Holy Ghost. In those first months, more people received the Holy Ghost in Mark's services than in mine. God used him in a way that was awesome, and he showed a spiritual maturity far beyond his years. He preached at the Liberian National Conference with an unction and power that brought sinners to the altar and the church to its knees, both preachers and laity.

When the rainy season begins each year, termites swarm at a certain time in the evening. The termites have wings and look like a flying larva or worm. Of course, they are attracted to a light at night. Consequently, at church, whether the light was a lantern or an electric bulb, the termites flew around it, multitudes of them. This made it difficult to preach, because the light was always in front of the preacher. So I preached and swatted, preached and swatted. The termites got in my hair, on my clothes, on my face, and on my Bible.

Strangely, after a while they would fall to the floor as they lost their wings; then they crawled all over the floor. Just when the situation would look hopeless, the termites would stop swarming and amazingly disappear just in time for the altar service.

It was a special day the first time we went to the historic Bomi Hills mission station. We had heard much about Bomi Hills ever since coming to the Lord.

We lived for two months in the very quarters on the mission station once occupied by Sister Valda Russell. Her favorite chair was still in the house.

We talked to people who were present when Missionary Jack Langham's daughter was shot to death. As I stood in the room where she died, I felt that I was standing on ground hallowed by the blood of spiritual pioneers, giants of faith who had dedicated themselves to reach the African people. I stood by the grave of this fine girl and thought of the sacrifice made by the Langham family. Every sacrifice had been made with love.

Brother Langham was not at home when his daughter was shot. When he reached the house later and heard about his daughter's death, the police brought the perpetrator to him. He was a young man who worked regularly on the mission compound and was well known to the Langham family. The man was deeply sorry and said it had been an accident. The Liberians wanted him to receive the greatest penalty allowed by law, but Brother Langham pleaded for him to be released and forgiven. Some of the Liberians told me that his display of Christian love changed their life and convinced them of the truth of the gospel of Jesus Christ.

I saw where Sam Latta's airplane crashed on the mission school's playground. Momentum carried it across the main road and into a store building. Brother Latta climbed out of the plane uninjured. No one else was injured either, but the plane was a total loss.

The roll call of missionaries who had served here was long. I thought of Mother Holmes, Pauline Gruse, Valda Russell, Ena Hylton, Laverne Collins, Gladys Robinson, Porter Davis, the Parks family, the Basil Williams family, the Cupples family, Brother and Sister Harvey Davis, Else Lund, the Garlands, Sister Bailey, and Brother and Sister Otis Petty.

I could not remember all the names and wished I could. A person did not have to be there but a few days to realize that these men, women, and children had made truly great sacrifices in giving themselves to the work of God for Liberia. And it is tragic for such sacrifice and service to go unremembered. The names of some of these missionaries to Liberia could well stand alongside the names of faithful heroes in Hebrews 11.

At the back of the Bomi Hills mission station were a number of undeveloped acres. Every day that I could, I would go there and spend hours alone walking through the trees praying, meditating, weeping and talking with God, asking Him to use us and give us souls. The Lord was wonderfully close as I walked with Him there. His words, "Go . . . and, lo, I am with you alway, even unto the end of the world" were precious to me. I held them as a personal promise.

When the time came for us to take a trip to Fassama we were excited. Fassama was just as famous as Bomi Hills, but much more remote. At that time, there were two ways to get there: you could walk for three days or charter a small plane to take you there. We were going to fly, thank God. Fifteen of us were going, so we needed two airplanes. On boarding, we separated the parents of each family to ensure that no children would be left as orphans in case one of the planes went down.

The passenger door of the plane I was on was tied

shut because the door catches were broken. My plane arrived first and we landed on the very short, uphill, uneven dirt airfield that was full of potholes. It was good to be on the ground again after flying above the vast green expanse of jungle that had never revealed a gap.

Because of the shortness of the airfield, the other plane had to land at a village about twenty miles away. Then our plane went to pick up the other passengers to bring them on to Fassama.

When Sister O'Keefe's turn came to disembark, she missed the step and fell towards the ground. Fortunately, the pastor of the mission, Joseph Yarkpai, caught her. We all had a good laugh, but it had been a tense flight low over an impenetrable jungle, a jungle so dense that a plane lost in it would be swallowed up as completely as if submerged in an ocean, never to be found again.

In Fassama, as in Bomi Hills, we felt surrounded by history. Here, Sister Laverne Collins had given her life. Just six months after her arrival in Liberia a malarial fever took her. Her grave site was a memorial to a life unselfishly laid down for her Master.

Sister Gruse had walked through this jungle to bring salvation here. She built the house that she lived in and that still stands—a round mud hut. Here, in front of many witnesses, she was killed by a bolt of lightning. As she lay dead on the ground, the villagers felt that their heathen gods had shown their power in striking down this purveyor of a strange new religion. But then something happened. Sister Gruse rose from the dead! She stood up! Healed! Alive!

The people were stunned. Her God was greater than all of theirs.

On another occasion, some villagers tried to kill one of the missionaries by putting a deadly cobra on her bed while she slept. The snake would not bite.

The next day the village witch doctors confessed that they had been trying to kill the missionary with the snake and with devil curses. They acknowledged the failure of their gods and admitted that Jesus Christ was greater. Revival came to Fassama.

I thought of Brother Harvey Davis, who contracted a case of amoebic dysentery, of the horrible suffering he experienced with what was at that time an incurable disease. He was sent back to America to die with his intestines destroyed. Conquering the powers of darkness required a high price. These pioneers paid that price.

Things were different now. A large mission station prospered that had trained many of the dedicated ministers who were now the national leaders of the United Pentecostal Church of Liberia. The sacrifices of Sister Gruse, Sister Collins, Brother Davis, and others were not in vain. What they built lives on now and shall forever more.

The next few days were restful. We thoroughly enjoyed the church services, the good African food, and the fellowship. Then, my son Tom was stricken with malaria, the same dreaded disease that had killed Laverne Collins at the same place. His fever raged for days. Fortunately, we had at the mission station some antimalarial medicine. Tom responded to the medicine and prayer and was soon well again. Thank God!

While at Fassama, a group of men and boys decided to hike ten miles to the next village to check on a radio transmitter. It was a relatively easy walk on a well-worn dirt trail with many little bridges to cross, if I dare call them bridges. Usually the bridge was just a single log stretched over a murky, scummy, disease-infested creek. Sometimes there would be a single shaky handrail, but usually there was none. You had to keep your balance or you would land in the creek. Several people slipped on these bridges but always managed to catch themselves in time until my son Mark slipped. He caught the log under him in a bear hug and a scissors grip, but instead of staying on top of the log, he slipped underneath it and briefly hung upside down. Then he lost his grip, dropped into the filthy, stagnant water, and disappeared beneath the surface. Fortunately, it wasn't deep, and Mark was soon standing, sputtering and spitting. He was completely soaked and thoroughly disgusted. We all broke up laughing; we couldn't help it. The gymnastics of his entrance into the creek were just too spectacular. Mark soon recovered his good humor and suffered no ill effects from his dunking.

As we continued our hike, we passed many long, thick vines hanging down from the high trees. I remembered from my boyhood stories of Tarzan swinging through the trees from vine to vine with a knife between his teeth. That gave me an idea: if Tarzan could do it, why not I? I selected a strong-looking vine, prepared myself to rend the jungle with the wild cry of the king of the apes, and then threw my weight onto the vine. The vine came loose from its moorings, and all sorts of jungle junk cascaded onto my head. By the time I finished brushing myself off and combing the debris out of my hair, I was thoroughly disillusioned with Edgar Rice Burroughs and his Tarzan. This time the group had a good laugh at my expense.

It is commonly said that you do not have to be crazy to be a missionary, but it helps.

After a few days, we left Fassama and flew back to Monrovia, and then were driven back to the house at Brewaville.

In February 1976 the United States Embassy invited us to a celebration of America's Independence Day. In the United States we had always observed the occasion on the Fourth of July, but in Liberia there is too much rain then. Consequently, Americans living in West Africa celebrate the day in February.

The prospects of seeing other Americans was, in itself, exciting. In addition, the embassy advertised that there would be a cookout with genuine American hot dogs and hamburgers.

Our group dressed for the occasion and made our way to the designated site for the festivities. The activities were loosely planned and casual. There was a lot of friendly chatter, meeting new people, and invariably the question "Where in the States are you from?" was asked when we made new acquaintances.

It is strange, but Americans in Africa begin feeling that another American in Africa is almost a relative. They become so isolated from American culture that the slightest sound of an American accent will draw them through a crowd to ask a stranger, "Are you an American?" The feeling of kinship with that stranger seems very real.

At the close of the Independence Day activities the American ambassador made a brief speech reminding us of the meaning of this observance. Then there was a drum roll, and we all stood to our feet as four uniformed U.S. Marines marched in with the Stars and Stripes. The flag was set in its stand, and the Marines held their salute at attention while we all repeated the Pledge of Allegiance. As we sang the national anthem, hundreds of us wept unashamed for love of the country we had left behind. Never in my life had I been so moved by a flag ceremony. Never before had I felt so patriotic. Rolling in my soul was the prayer and the song "God Bless America."

I have come to the conclusion that no group on earth can sing that song with greater feeling than American foreign missionaries. There was a lump in my throat and an ache in my heart. It was not that I wanted to leave Africa, definitely not. I was there in the will of God and considered my missionary calling as the highest honor in my life. Still I loved and missed America, my country.

While we were still in Liberia I was introduced to a young man who was a citizen of Sierra Leone. He had not been in Liberia long. He had gone to America to attend a technical college, but had had difficulties with his studies, had dropped out of college, and was therefore deported. He was ashamed to return to his family in Sierra Leone, so he came instead to Liberia. While in Liberia he met Brother Albert Stewart, who converted him from Islam to Christianity.

This young man was in dire straits. He knew no one, had no money, and had no place to live. The missionaries took him under their wing, gave him a job as a tutor for the three youngest missionary children, and gave him a place to live.

He was congenial and intelligent, and we took a strong liking to him. Inasmuch as he was a Sierra Leonean, we hoped that he would be able to open doors for the gospel in Sierra Leone. At that time, we had no idea of the various roles he would play in our life and in the work of God in Sierra Leone.

TWO

WE WERE APPOINTED as missionaries to Sierra Leone, West Africa, in 1974. Our stay in Liberia was to be brief and to serve as an orientation to West Africa. Liberia was considered the best place to apply for resident visas for Sierra Leone. In our efforts to get these visas I made five trips into Sierra Leone, going through a bureaucratic maze that would have been hilarious if it had not been so frustrating. Reasons given to me for long delays were as follows: "The vice president is out of the country and nothing can be done until he returns." "Visiting dignitaries are with the head of state, so you must wait." "The principal immigration officer is on vacation." "We have had holidays." "We cannot find your application."

My first trip into Sierra Leone was especially memorable. Denzil Bolton, a missionary appointed to Liberia, a young Liberian church member named David Momoh, and I flew to Sierra Leone's international airport, Lungi. The airport building was little more than a shack alongside a runway. From the airport we caught a bus to Freetown, the capital city.

Between the airport and Freetown is the mouth of a large river that must be crossed on a ferry boat. The river is about five miles wide at this point, and the trip across usually takes about forty-five minutes.

Unfortunately, the ferries are old and unreliable, and

the trip schedules don't mean much. It is common to wait hours for a ferry to show up. Although the airport is only twenty-five miles from Freetown, a trip there and back usually takes a whole day.

The ferry was big enough to carry thirty to forty cars plus hundreds of people afoot. Most of the pedestrian passengers were carrying heavy loads of produce or dried fish to the markets in Freetown. Walking up and down on the ferry were people selling gum, candy, cookies, and even pieces of roasted meat on a skewer.

On the upper deck a pleasant breeze gave relief from the constant heat, and the view in all directions was beautiful. Looking toward the dock on the far shore, we could see Freetown. It seemed to be stretched out in a long line made necessary by the terrain. On the north and west, the Sierra Leone River and the Atlantic Ocean formed city limits, but on the south, serving as a back-drop to the city, were the mountains that gave the country its name: Sierra Leone. The name is Portuguese, and it means "Lion Mountain" or "Mountain of the Lion." They were beautiful, yet steep and rugged. They were true mountains, not just high hills, but their spectacular rise and ruggedness seemed softened by the blanket of jungle foliage that covered them from base to peak.

Mountain of the Lion. The name was descriptive and proved to be prophetic.

As the ferry drew near land to dock, the market mamas, as many of them were called, were the first people on or off, often walking through shallow water before the ferry was fully docked.

Our bus took us into Freetown to the Paramount Hotel, a no-star facility with four-star prices. But the hotel was well situated in the center of town and convenient for our purposes.

Early the next morning we made our way to the

Department of Immigration to apply for resident visas for my family and me. We filled out all the forms and gave photos and other requested documents along with our passports. We were told to return in a few days to check on the progress of our applications.

We had time on our hands, so we wandered around familiarizing ourselves with the people and the layout of the town.

Although Sierra Leone borders Liberia and some of the tribes indigenous to Sierra Leone are also indigenous to Liberia, the two countries are markedly different in many ways. Whereas Liberia was influenced by America during the colonial period, Sierra Leone was a British colony until 1961, when it gained its independence. The British culture has left its imprint on its former colonies, at least in a superficial way.

Only ten percent of the Sierra Leoneans speak English, but those who do, speak it with a British accent. The laws follow the British judicial system for the most part, and the government makes a pretense of following a parliamentary system. The architecture of the homes in the city is decidedly that of the British during the colonial period. These homes are small two-story wooden structures that suffer the ravages of an equatorial climate and the onslaughts of the most voraciously active termite population in the world. They are built very close together, and the wood is as dry as dust. Consequently, when fires do break out, it is common for four or five homes to burn before the fire can be brought under control.

The people of Sierra Leone speak twenty different languages, the most prominent of which are Mende, Temne, Limba, Lokko, Kroo, Sherbro, Fullah, Mandingo, Susu, Vai, Gola, Gissie, Koronko, Kono, Creole, and English. The lingua franca is Creole; in most places people speak it in addition to their tribal dialect. Although this Creole has an English base, it is totally incomprehensible to an untrained American ear. And being alone in a place where everyone else speaks a foreign language leaves a person feeling isolated, dependent, and vulnerable.

Local taxis are designated by a yellow license plate. They have no meters, so fares must be agreed upon before you enter. The fare rises and falls according to the weather, time of day, current price of gasoline, age of vehicle, attitude of the driver, appearance and attitude of the passenger, and so on.

When a person does get a taxi, he does not have exclusive rights to it. The driver will continue to pick up as many other people going in the same general direction as the car can hold. That means at least four in the back seat and three or four in the front seat of a little Mazda or Nissan.

Anyway, we caught a taxi to cruise around in. The streets were narrow and filled with potholes. In some places the gutters were deep ditches with a vertical dropoff immediately next to the driving lane and with no curbs to keep cars from falling into them. Kiosks lined the streets everywhere. The smell of the markets was that of rotting vegetation and fermentation. We labeled it "Lily of the Alley."

Traffic was heavy, and even the main street of town, Siaka Stevens Street, was only a two-lane road. People parked anywhere and everywhere—the sidewalk, in the road, on the wrong side of the road—anywhere.

A couple days later we went back to check on our visa applications. There was no progress! They had not done a thing! They now told me that I would have to apply in a different manner at another location to different people at another time. One of the first things that you learn in West Africa is to exercise considerable patience in dealing with the bureaucracy. I thanked them for their kindness and asked them to advise me of the correct way to proceed. I was told that I would have to apply to the office of the national vice president but that he was out of the country and would not be back for a number of days. I could not apply at this time. I would have to return to Liberia, get another visitor's visa, and then return to Sierra Leone at a future date to apply again for residence permits.

Inasmuch as our visitor's visas would expire before the vice president's return, and inasmuch as I could not leave our passports there for our applications to be processed in our absence, I picked them up to travel back to Liberia. Anyway, the next day was Christmas Eve, and we all wanted to get back to our families by then.

We spent the night at the Paramount Hotel and left early the next morning for the bus stop. You have never been to a bus stop like this. Always there are many more people to ride on the bus than there are seats. The lines form before sunup, hours before the buses come.

When the buses showed up at 8:00 A.M., the lines disintegrated. Total chaos ensued. There was pushing, cursing, and fist fights. It was just short of a riot. I still don't understand how, but we got on that bus. God must have been with us. We weren't even hurt.

The bus ride was the best part of our trip back to Liberia. The bus stayed on paved roads for 150 miles and then let us off at the second-largest town in the country, Bo.

From Bo it was all downhill as far as comfort was concerned. We haggled to get a ride on what is known as a poda-poda, which is like a van with benches in it. The poda-poda took us to Kenema, another well-known town about forty miles from Bo.

In Kenema, we found a man with an open station

wagon who would drive us and several other people to the border for a fee. It was dirt road all the way. Every window of the vehicle stayed open all the way to the border in spite of the clouds of dust being sucked through the windows. This leg of the journey lasted about five and a half hours. We arrived at the border about 8:00 P.M.

The border is the Mano River. We knew we were late to make a crossing, so the driver drove to the bank of the river and began flashing his headlights while the rest of us yelled across the river for the canoes to come for us. They had just been leaving for the night. Thankfully the canoes came back. We slid down the muddy bank to the river with our luggage in hand. While carrying one of the suitcases, the driver slipped and fell flat on his back. The suitcase broke open, scattering clothes in the mud. Quickly we stuffed everything back in the suitcase and loaded our things and ourselves into the canoes, thankful that we would not have to spend the night on the river bank.

On the other side of the river, a little Japanese pickup truck with benches in its bed was waiting for us. It took us to the Liberian customs station, where the customs agent was playing a game of checkers.

As our group of fifteen wayfarers approached him with our travel documents, he ignored us. He was playing checkers, and we would have to wait until the game was finished.

When his game was over he looked up and acknowledged our existence. Then he looked at his watch and said, "It is after eight o'clock. Customs is closed. You will have to spend the night here." We were all exhausted and there was no place to sleep but the ground or the wooden porch.

The people pleaded with him. They said, "You must let us pass." This offended the agent. He said, "I don't have to do anything," got up, and walked off into the night. Immediately, the travelers followed him begging him to forgive them for saying that he "must" do anything. They begged him to let them pass and began to give him money. When he was sufficiently mollified, he returned and processed our papers and we were on our way once again.

We boarded the little pickup again. It passed through terrain that had no right to be called a road with bushes scraping both sides of the truck. We passed through ditches and holes so deep that it seemed that we might turn over. We had to hang on strongly lest one of the jarring bumps toss us completely out of the truck. When we finally reached Brewaville, where the families had gathered for Christmas Eve, it was midnight. Everybody had waited up for us, and there was a very happy reunion. They were glad that we were back and we were glad to be back. I was so exhausted that I felt sick, and we were so filthy that it was a wonder our families could recognize us. The dirt was so thick on us that they could hardly tell who were the black passengers and who were the white ones. Anyway, we had made it home for Christmas.

We made four more trips into Sierra Leone before we succeeded in getting our resident visas. Finally, after five months of pleading, cajoling, encouraging, and pushing, the resident visas were in my hand.

THREE

I<small>T WAS A HAPPY</small> and exciting day when I returned to Liberia to show my wife, Abbie, the visas. At last, we could move into Sierra Leone and begin our work.

Our young Sierra Leonean friend decided to join us and return to his country. We decided that he, Mark, and I would travel overland to Freetown, acquire a house, clear our shipment of furniture and goods through customs at the port, and get the house set up to live in.

It was an exhausting week. At that time, there were no real estate offices in the country. We located a home to rent by driving around until we saw an unoccupied house. Then we asked the neighbors if they knew the owner, if they had his address, and if the house would be rented. The prospective renter had to use his initiative at every level to come up with a lease for a house. God was with me, and we were able to acquire a ten-year lease on a home in a good area.

Then our shipment of goods arrived in port. We had to move quickly to avoid demurrage charges. Clearing customs was an unbelievable hassle. It took three days of haggling with various agents. The port is a large area stretching about one mile from end to end, and I felt as if I made the round trip about ten times each of those three days.

One of the problems centered around two .22-caliber

rifles belonging to my two older sons. These were confiscated along with all the ammunition for them. I had not realized how strict Sierra Leone was on the possession of personal firearms. Unfortunately, much of Africa has a history of coups as the means of changing political leadership. Consequently, firearms are tightly controlled.

Finally, after we had paid the required customs fees and cleared our way through the last of the red tape, we got our crates loaded on the back of a flatbed truck and headed for our new home.

Getting the truck unloaded and everything moved into the house was hard work in the heat and humidity, especially since the house had an awkward access to the entrance that made getting everything into it difficult. Mark, our friend, and I worked from early until late every day to get everything set into its proper place.

Then I sent word to Abbie to fly into Sierra Leone with our two younger sons, Tom and Don. I picked them up at the airport and brought them to their new home.

I was anticipating her pleasure in seeing her home set up, but when we entered the house she sat down, looked around, and then broke into tears. Of course, her tears upset me and our boys. I did not know what was wrong. We had tried so hard to fix things up right because we wanted her to be happy. We had gone without food and sleep and worked until we were worn out to get the house ready for her, and now she was crying. Then, through her tears, she explained that she was not upset or disappointed; she was crying because she was happy—happy to see her furniture and personal things, happy to have a home.

We had been without a home for a year and a half. Part of the time we had been traveling in North America to raise the funds to come to Africa, but we had spent the last five months in Liberia. When we lived in Bomi

Hills, we did not have a stove, a refrigerator, a washing machine, or a bed for our sons. We did not have enough chairs to sit on. We lacked electricity and often we were without water.

Now, we had a refrigerator, a stove, a washing machine, a dryer, chairs, and beds, but most important, we had a home again. To us it seemed like a sanctuary, a place for privacy, a place that was ours, even if it was being leased. It was more than a house; it was our home.

Abbie—I often call her Mama—is a good wife and mother. She is serious about seeing that her family has a clean, attractive, and well-organized home. Although, Mark, our friend, and I had set up the basic furniture, there was much still to be done. Mama dove into the job, putting a woman's touch everywhere—on the walls, kitchen counters, curtains, and so on.

It was a good feeling to have a home again, not to feel like a vagabond constantly dependent upon the charity of others for a table to eat at and a bed to sleep in. People had been very good to us, very kind and hospitable, but there is a comfort and a liberty that can only be had in your own home. We now had a home and we thanked God for it.

Our first nights in our new home were unsettling at times. We were awakened quite a few times by groups of drunk men passing the house and singing loudly in the middle of the night. More unsettling than the drunks was the occasional sound of guns being fired. We often peeked out the windows wondering what was going on.

After a few days, the neighbors told us the guns were being fired at roving bands of thieves ready almost nightly to break into the homes of the unwary. We learned to sleep lightly.

The very next morning, Abbie arose early, and as she walked towards the living room, she heard the crash of breaking glass from a door that served as an entrance from a veranda. Next, a hand appeared through the door reaching where a key would be if it had been left in the lock. Abbie shouted at the would-be thief, prompting him to make a quick getaway.

That glass door had metal bars crisscrossing it to prevent entry, and we had not left the key in the lock, but the incident nevertheless served to keep us alert.

The need for security faced everyone who had anything worth stealing. In our area, every home had an eight-foot cement wall surrounding it. The top of this wall was invariably imbedded with broken glass, every window had steel bars, and all doors had double or triple locks. Nothing of value could be left outside a locked enclosure, including any vehicles. In addition, every home had guards both day and night. We had two guards at night and one in the day. We never left our home unattended.

Yet, all these precautions could not guarantee security from thieves. Quite often the guard is the inside man who sets up a break-in. Consequently, when a break-in is reported to the police, they automatically arrest the guard. The guard is locked up in a cell that has no lights, water, bed, or bathroom facilities.

The guard may be innocent, but a large percent of break-ins prove to involve the guard. Still, not to have a guard would almost assure the loss of one's goods. So owners strive to find good guards and maintain a good relationship with them.

Our first guard was an old man whom we knew as Pa Sam. His job was to guard the house at night. He sat in a chair on the front veranda and was supposed to walk around the house periodically to be sure that all was well.

The problem was that Pa Sam always fell asleep when

he was supposed to be guarding. In fact, he slept better than we did. I devised a system to keep him awake: I hung a large piece of iron from a tree branch in our back yard and told him he was to hit it every hour on the hour during the night. Pa Sam threatened to quit rather than sound my improvised gong, but I held my ground and he finally conceded. I thought I had won the argument, but I was wrong.

That night after we were all asleep, Pa Sam took up his duties. At midnight he hit the gong, and hit it and hit it and hit it. He beat on that gong for about twenty minutes, until all the neighbors were awake and threatening to call the police. Finally, he stopped.

Around one in the morning he started again. I realized that I had not won. Pa Sam was demonstrating his displeasure with his new duty. I had a choice: I could fire him, I could insist that he continue to observe the new rule and expose myself to charges of disturbing the peace, or I could remove my gong and let Pa Sam go back to sleep. I removed the gong.

My son Mark has more than his share of mischief in him. Once, he disguised himself as a thief and walked up to our sleeping guard. He shook the old man to wake him and told him to turn over the keys to the house or he would kill him. Well, Pa Sam did not have the keys and began to beg for his life. Finally, Mark began laughing and revealed himself.

Of course, Pa Sam never admitted to sleeping. You could walk up and take his flashlight, sandals, and cutlass, then accuse him of sleeping and he would deny it. When you presented him with the evidence, he would mumble and sulk, and when you left, return to his sleep. As a guard he was hopeless. Still we all liked the old man.

The worst trick ever played on Pa Sam was perpetrated by Mark and Kevin Blake, the son of Brother and

Sister Larry Blake, missionaries to Liberia. Kevin was spending a week with us in Sierra Leone, and because he and Mark were close in age, they spent a lot of time together. Between them they concocted a plot to play a trick on the old man.

As usual, Pa Sam was asleep. Kevin went down the stairs below the veranda carrying an empty Pringles canister and took up a position just out of sight. Then Mark, carrying a BB gun, came out on the veranda and began to yell, "Thief, thief, thief!" He raised the gun, aimed, and right on cue Kevin, from his position below the veranda, squeezed the empty Pringles canister. The canister made a loud bang, then Mark yelled, "I got him! I got him!"

By now Pa Sam was wide awake and intent on saving his life from thieves and guns. Instead of standing fast to protect us and our property, he took off running for a safe place to hide. Unfortunately, he slipped on the first turn and skinned his knee, but with fear motivating him and adrenaline pushing him, he was back on his feet right away going full speed. He made it down the stairs and through a passage leading to the back of the house. Here he made a right turn and headed for a place of safety among some bushes, but as he neared the corner of the garage Kevin stepped out of the darkness. When Pa Sam saw him, he thought he was the thief. Pa Sam wet himself.

At this point the boys broke up laughing. Pa Sam wasn't laughing. He kept saying, "E na weekid bobo." (He is a wicked boy.)

Of course, I had to put a stop to the boys' mischief. Strangely enough, Pa Sam really liked Mark. Ten years after Mark had left Africa, Pa Sam would still ask how he was doing.

In any case, we felt we needed a guard who would not sleep. If he slept, we could not. So we had to let Pa Sam go.

Our boys were getting their education through correspondence courses. Don's course especially required a teacher's assistance, so our Sierra Leonean friend became Don's tutor. This arrangement continued satisfactorily for years. The boys settled into a schedule of school work during the day and getting acquainted with the new surroundings and new friends in the evenings and on weekends.

We had to learn our way around town, where to find goods and services. There were only two ways from our house to town. One was a bottom road, the main road, that held most of the traffic, and the other was a scenic route through the mountains. Inasmuch as we did not have a car, we would have to walk from the house about half a mile to a place where we could catch a taxi. We did not buy a vehicle during the five months we were in Liberia because we always considered our stay there temporary. In addition, we would have had to pay duty on it if we later took it to Sierra Leone. It was another two months after moving into Sierra Leone before we were able to get a car, so we were seven months without a car.

It was a happy day when we did get a car. I could not get one with an air conditioner in it, and it would have cost two thousand dollars for a little ineffective add-on unit. It was too much for too little, so I chose to do without the air conditioner.

We had a telephone installed. I don't know why, because it was totally useless. It was out of order as much as it was in order. I would attempt to call town thirty-five to forty times without success. Finally, I would give up, get in the car, and drive the seven miles to tend to whatever I had hoped to handle on the telephone. Many times I could not even call my neighbor's house.

Usually, when the telephone was not working, which was at least once a week, it would not be long before the telephone repairman would be at our door. He knew my phone wasn't working before I did, which is not surprising, because he would climb up the telephone pole and disconnect us. Then he would knock on our door to notify us that our telephone was out of order and that he could fix it for a fee. He would check our telephone and, sure enough, it wouldn't be working. I should not have been surprised, for it didn't work even when it was working. Anyway, the repairman came in and tightened or loosened a few screws and said that it would soon begin working again. And he was right. Why, that phone began working just as soon as he climbed back up the pole and reconnected our line! This became a weekly ritual. It was a system of paying our dues in order to keep a useless telephone. Finally, we gave up and removed the telephone, counting it a lost cause.

We moved into our home in April 1976, the hottest time of the year. We were beginning to get acclimated, but somewhere along the years I began to realize that I would never really get used to the heat and humidity.

We laughingly tell people that we have two seasons in Sierra Leone—hot and hotter. Actually, there are two seasons—the dry season and the rainy season—but they are both hot.

The Sierra Leoneans are used to this consistent heat. If the temperature drops to eighty degrees, they are cold and want to build a fire. If the temperature drops below eighty degrees, people everywhere get sick. They bear the heat well but have very little ability to withstand lower temperatures. When I tried to describe winter in parts of the world that have snow and ice, it was hard for them to envision such conditions.

The rainy season usually begins the first part of June.

And that beginning is spectacular, sometimes even awesome. Never in my life had I seen such storms—rain falling in blinding torrents; thunder so loud it seemed that bombs were exploding; lightning striking everywhere with the frequency of a metronome, lighting both earth and sky with a bluish white brilliance and leaving behind it the smell of scorched ozone. But it was the force of the wind that was most awesome. Huge trees were uprooted, branches were broken off, roofs were taken from buildings, deadly debris flew through the air, and rain moved horizontally. Every year these storms came.

These first rainstorms came with such a high pressure that water literally found its way through boards. It would come through crevasses so small that it seemed impossible, and it did not just seep through, it shot horizontally into the room as if it were coming out of a toy water pistol.

The worst storms hit at night, suddenly, with full force. There was no staying in bed. Immediately, my wife and I were out of bed, because we knew water was going to come into the house. Furniture and carpets had to be moved.

And since it was normal to be without electricity, it was pitch dark in the house. We had to get candles or flashlights going. Sometimes the force of the wind penetrating our house kept the candle flames flickering.

Once we moved the furniture and carpets, we manned the mops, towels, and water buckets. To mop up ten gallons of water in a storm was not unusual. It was a frantic effort to get the water up as fast as it came in. Sometimes we did not keep up, and water was everywhere.

Then, just as suddenly as the storm had begun it would stop, leaving devastation behind.

We would clean up all that we could and crawl back into bed in the wee hours of the morning knowing that the next night would bring another storm. These violent storms usually came nightly for three to four weeks.

Then in July, August, September, and October, it rained and rained and rained. There was plenty of lightning and thunder, but the wind was gone.

We had two dogs, Bucky and Pierre. When the thunder boomed, the dogs trembled from head to foot. There was no consoling them. They wanted a place to hide. They were terrified.

We received about two hundred inches of rain each year. About mid November the rains would stop. Then December and January would bring us the finest weather of the year.

Sometime in January the phenomenon called harmattan would take place. It was a cloud of brown dust that came from the Sahara Desert, covering the sky from horizon to horizon. It would cover many countries and hundreds of thousands of square miles. Sometimes it was so thick that we could not see the sun and ground level visibility was reduced to one hundred yards.

This dust hung in the air for two to three months, through February, March, and into April. It covered everything. We would breathe it and eat it. It invaded everything. We could not close our home or our car tight enough to keep it out. The dust, as fine as the finest silt, covered our furniture, our floors, our dishes—everything. We would clean it up and an hour later it was as if nothing had been done; again the dust covered everything.

Through each season—dry, rainy, harmattan, no matter which—it was intolerably hot and humid. There was no cool season of respite or relief, no time of escape from the oppressive climate, no time to revitalize one's system.

Nighttime was the worst, because the walls of the house were made of cement blocks and retained the heat of the day. Because of the mosquitoes we could not open the windows, and it would not have helped a great deal if we had. Although the nights were cooler than the days, they were still warm.

When I went to bed I wore no pajamas, not even a T-shirt. I did not put so much as a sheet over me. Still I would lie there and sweat all night until the bottom sheet was wet and my body was slick with sweat.

We did have an air conditioner, which was a tremendous blessing. When we had electricity we would turn it on and bask in the glory of its cool air.

No story about Sierra Leone would be complete without some comments about its mosquito population. Some people refer to the mosquito as the national bird of the country. The mosquitoes are everywhere.

The mosquitoes are spreaders of disease, the most notorious being malaria, the greatest killer disease in the world. On the African continent, over two million people die from malaria every year. Somehow many people in America have the mistaken idea that the natives of Africa are immune to malaria. Nobody is born with an immunity to this deadly disease, and neither does surviving a case of malaria give a person immunity from future attacks.

Nobody likes mosquitoes. It is a terrible thing for me to turn out the light at night, lie down on my bed, and then hear the droning song of a marauding blood sucker. Because it is so hot, I cannot hide under the covers or a sheet.

The mosquito makes a probing attack at my ear. I make some ineffectual slaps at my ear. Of course, I miss him and hit myself, just as my antagonist intended. This probing action is repeated several times with the same response and the same result.

I get nervous and tense. Sleep is out of the question. My situation is untenable. Tactics must be changed. With a groan I roll out of bed. Determination sets in. "I'm going to get him!" The killer instinct takes over. The prey becomes the hunter.

How to locate him? He is a master in the art of camouflage, in knowing where and how to hide. The deadly game is set in motion: hunting and being hunted.

We turn on the best source of light at hand: a flashlight, a candle, or sometimes a lantern. Then, armed with a swatter or a bug bomb, I painstakingly, inch by inch, search the shadows and crevasses, moving in such a way as not to alert him should I discover his hiding place. I am hoping that he will make a mistake and outline himself against a light background, or maybe he will fly out of cover.

When I find him I have to be ready. I must be sure the bug bomb is facing the right direction. When I flush him out I will probably get only one shot at him. If I miss him he will conceal himself in a place doubly hard to locate the next time. If I do not find him and kill him, he will come after us again when the lights go out.

The primitive call of the hunter excites my blood. The tension builds as I close in on the quarry. Abbie shouts, "There he is on the wall!" Fearlessly, I make my approach, aiming the bug bomb carefully. Something in my approach alarms him! He takes flight! Desperately I begin firing, hoping to knock him out of the air. I think of the antiaircraft guns trying to bring down the bombers in World War II. I fire again and again. Aha, I've got him enveloped in a cloud of insecticide! He falters in flight and falls to the bed! He's down! He's down! I've won!

I swagger over to the corpse, relieved. We got him. We are safe now. We will be able to sleep unmolested. I pick him up by the wings and, without any remorse, flush him down the toilet.

We turn out the lights and return to bed. Then Abbie says, "I can't sleep. That insecticide smell is gagging me."

FOUR

REVEREND R. E. S. NYANMOH was about seventy years old when I first met him. I say "about" because the majority of people in Sierra Leone do not know when they were born nor, consequently, their age. He was of the Kroo tribe, which is known for the aggressiveness and strength of its people. He was about five feet two inches tall and had a disconcerting way of batting his eyes up and down when endeavoring to make a flowery speech, which was quite often.

His wife, Sister Nyanmoh, was older than he, about seventy-three. She was about four feet nine inches tall and weighed about eighty pounds. She was afflicted with Parkinson's disease, which caused her body to shake all the time.

The two of them lived in an apartment building. This building was a one story rectangle about twelve feet wide and about forty feet long that was divided into five separate apartments each twelve feet by eight feet. Each small apartment was then divided to make two rooms each about six feet by eight feet. The back room of Brother and Sister Nyanmoh's apartment was their bedroom. The front room was the living room, dining room, and additional bedroom.

The walls and the roof were covered with rusty corrugated sheets of thin metal, and windows were cut through the metal for air flow. In front of the entrance was mud and stagnant water that never seemed to dry up. There was no electricity, water, or bathroom facilities. Water and an outhouse were available at community sites.

Of course, there was no place to cook in the apartment. Over ninety-five percent of all cooking in Sierra Leone takes place outdoors over an open wood fire. That is how Sister Nyanmoh cooked.

They had never had children of their own, so they took in two boys to raise. These boys were not orphans. In fact, their parents, who were related to Brother and Sister Nyanmoh, were quite able to raise the boys themselves. I knew that the Nyanmohs were desperately poor and could not afford to feed and clothe themselves let alone two boys, so I asked Brother Nyanmoh why he did not let their parents raise them. He said, "Brother O'Keefe, I cannot afford it, but I must do it. It is our culture. My sister has sent them to me to raise, so I just have to do it."

I asked, "Do they give you something to help feed them?"

He answered, "No, they do not give anything. I must be responsible. If I do not raise them, it will be a shame to me." There is a lot to learn in a new culture, and I was beginning to learn.

These people lived with a degree of poverty known to few in America, yet they were generous in their hospitality to my wife and me. I ate their food and slept on the bed in their living room. The food was always rice with a sauce made of palm oil, greens, and pepper. It was tasty but hot enough to make my eyeballs sweat, or maybe that was tears. Extremely hot food is something else for which the Kroo tribe is known. In any case, they were giving their best to us out of kindness and generosity.

The bed was not as hard as a rock, but it only missed by a few degrees.

Brother Nyanmoh pastored a little group of Kroo people in a little shack located on Guy Street in Freetown. Counting all the adults and children, there were about twenty members in the group.

This was the first place in which I preached in Sierra Leone. Every service was by candlelight; there was no electricity. The building was infested with rats that ran back and forth during the service. The rats did not seem to mind our being there, but they were distracting for Abbie.

The singing was quite nasal, and the music consisted of a crude drum or tambourine played with a strange, erratic beat peculiar to the Kroo tribe. The Kroo love their music and singing, and they feel that it is superior to that of other tribes.

I first met Brother and Sister Nyanmoh in December 1975, when I made my first excursion into Sierra Leone trying to obtain resident visas. He had been with an organization that seemed to have no clear teaching on the nature of God or His plan of salvation, and holiness was seldom, if ever, mentioned. He came out from them with a little group of people who desperately wanted direction from God. None of them had the Holy Ghost, but as I preached night after night they were filled with God's Spirit. They were ready. They were hungry for the Word of God.

As I preached to them, nobody said, "Amen" or demonstrated agreement, nor was there any worship. They were listening.

I could feel freedom and anointing as I preached, even though the people just listened quietly. I could not help but wonder if I was really getting through to them.

I finished preaching and it was time to pray. Then

that undemonstrative little group threw their hands up toward God and began to call on the name of the Lord Jesus Christ. As they prayed, some fell out on the floor and several received the Holy Ghost.

It was a wonderful service. They so wanted the truth. It was so refreshing to see the openness and simple faith of this little group meeting in this shack.

They wanted God. They wanted to be saved. And they wanted to become part of the United Pentecostal Church. We received the people as they received the new birth, and that little group meeting at Guy Street became the first United Pentecostal congregation in the nation of Sierra Leone.

During and after the service, I noticed, as I looked out the doors that were kept open for air, that many people were in the street listening to the service and many others were on the church steps. In subsequent services we would go out and persuade the people to come inside. Many times we would preach from the church steps to crowds that numbered into the hundreds. The people stood throughout the preaching and then openly, publicly, unashamed, in the street they would lift their hands and pray. Some would go down on their knees in prayer. Some received the Holy Ghost right there in the street.

There was an outhouse immediately adjacent to the church, and on the other side, right on the church steps, not ten feet from the main entrance, there was the smell of rotting vegetation from the markets selling cassava and oranges. No matter which way the wind blew, we were exposed to the rich, ripe odors of our surroundings.

Yet, in spite of every negative adjective that could have been used to describe the conditions of the people and the facilities, Jesus, our wonderful Lord, was there saying through the Spirit, "I love you. I died for you. I will adopt you and make you Mine."

Brother and Sister Nyanmoh walked to and from church. They had never owned a car, a motorcycle, or even a bicycle. They never would. I do not believe Sister Nyanmoh ever owned a pair of shoes, but Brother Nyanmoh had some used ones that somebody had given to him.

A start had been made for God in Sierra Leone. Our first converts! Our first church! Born in poverty and obscurity among the lowly, the uneducated, the backward, and the primitive. But there was shouting on the streets of glory as angels beheld a victory. The light of the glorious gospel of Jesus Christ had invaded the darkness of one more nation en route to the fulfillment of the prophecy stating, "This gospel of the kingdom shall be preached in all the world for a witness unto all nations; and then shall the end come." Hallelujah!

FIVE

WHILE GETTING SETTLED into our home, we had been preaching at Brother Nyanmoh's church, but as soon as we could we began to reach out to open new works. With Brother Nyanmoh and the young Sierra Leonean man who had come with us from Liberia, we began to seek open doors to preach wherever possible. Mark and the young man were my constant companions in evangelization. We went all over the country together.

One day the young man declared that God had called him to preach, so I began to train him in every way that I could. He went through different courses of study, getting high marks for comprehension. I spent a lot of time teaching him lesson after lesson, and he was getting a lot of practical training. In the early days, he was my main interpreter. Every time I preached a message in English, he preached the same message in a tribal dialect. He was at my side almost continually, observing, listening, learning, and practicing. He learned fast and seemingly became an invaluable asset in expanding the work of God in Sierra Leone.

The young man went to an area of Freetown called Dworzak Farm. It consisted of a single dirt road that led into a canyon with shabby homes and shacks rising on the canyon walls on both right and left. A polluted creek ran down the canyon, and nobody dared drink its water.

The only drinkable water in the settlement came from a single spigot located by a marketplace that sold the locally grown produce. Every day people waited in line at the spigot with their buckets. Once they had their buckets full they had to carry them up the canyon to their homes, maybe as much as three-fourths of a mile.

Africans don't carry loads as Americans do. They put the load on their heads. They can carry very heavy loads like this. If three men can lift a load onto a man's head, he can carry it. They have an amazing sense of balance when carrying these loads. I have seen women carry a bucket of water on their head and never spill a drop, even though they were walking over rough, rocky, and uneven terrain. And they never put a hand to the bucket to steady it.

In the middle of this settlement was a large Methodist Church building. The pastor was a fine old man who gave us permission to hold services in the church three times each week. Our services were separate from the Methodist services and conducted at different times.

We distributed flyers announcing our services and walked all over the canyon telling people. We talked about it in the marketplace and generally made people aware of our plans.

From the very beginning God blessed this work. The altars were always full of people. Sometimes there were so many seeking the Lord that it was impossible to get through the crowds to pray for all of them.

Many began to come for baptism. Sometimes we would hike up a steep, winding trail to a pond in the creek that was deep enough to baptize in. Other times, we would load people into our Peugeot station wagon and drive down to the ocean.

I always felt better about baptizing people in the

ocean because I had greater confidence that the water was safe. Much of the water in the interior of the country—rivers, swamps, creeks, and ponds—was infected with dangerous diseases like cholera and schistosomiasis. There were also crocodiles and poisonous snakes to think about. In Sierra Leone we learned to pray before we entered the water to baptize someone.

Baptismal services were always exciting, because there was usually a good number to be baptized—sometimes fifteen, twenty, thirty or thirty-five. There was usually a crowd of spectators, so we preached from the water's edge or from within the water to the gathered crowd.

Our congregation grew until we had more people than the Methodists. The numbers reached four hundred, with standing room only. This caused some resentment among the Methodists, but their pastor controlled them and continued to encourage us.

Next, the Sierra Leonean man we had met in Liberia opened a work in a village thirty-seven miles into the interior called Songo. Again, God blessed the work.

We began services in a little structure that served as a school for primary children. The benches were very low since they were built for little children.

Every Tuesday night we drove into Songo on an extremely rough road. The constant jarring due to potholes in the road was enough to destroy the shock absorbers and suspension on a vehicle, give a person a headache, or make him literally sick to his stomach.

When we reached the village, we would drive down the dirt main street with loudspeakers, announcing the service and preaching the gospel. The people gathered from everywhere into the dark little schoolroom. We set out candles or put up a lantern if we had one. The people loved the Pentecostal songs and worship. The services were good, and soon the room was packed.

When people were ready for baptism, we had to walk down a dark trail at night to water about a kilometer away. Abbie has a terrible fear of snakes, so she stepped high all the way there and back. The baptismal pool was stagnant and unhealthy looking, but the Lord kept His hand on us again and again as we entered diseased water to bury people in His name.

A notable miracle took place in Songo. One of the founding members of the congregation died at home. He was not breathing and his heart had stopped beating. There was no pulse. His family and some of the other new Christians began to pray for him. They prayed for five hours for God to raise him up. Then, through the power of the living God, breath came again into that dead man. The spark of life was renewed and he got up! He walked around glorifying God. He and those at the prayer meeting testified of the resurrection power of Jesus Christ.

The next door that opened was in Bo, the second-largest town in the country with a population of 50,000. We began holding services in a structure known as a court barrie. This is a building without any sides on it, just a floor and some pillars holding up a roof, used to conduct tribal court cases. Nearly every village had a court barrie, and there we often began services in a village.

In Bo, the court barrie was large and located right on a main road. Consequently, many outside the barrie heard the sound of our worship and the preaching of the Word. Many gathered to these services, and we soon had a faithful group of baptized followers meeting regularly in Bo.

To maintain this work we had to make a five-hour trip over bad roads every week. We went there every Saturday and returned late Sunday night or Monday.

We were reasonably pleased with the work, but the trips were leaving me exhausted. I was either eating food with bacteria in it that my system had not adjusted to, or I was hardly eating at all. During my first three years in Sierra Leone, I was sick after every trip I made to the interior. After every trip I had to spend a day or two in bed recovering. I made those trips at least once every week and sometimes twice. I never had so much sickness in my whole life. Sometimes it was dysentery, sometimes it was malaria, and sometimes we did not know what it was.

An intelligent young man out of Brother Nyanmoh's church, Torboh Johnson, was transferred by his job to Bo. After a couple of years he became the pastor and we were able to turn the work over to him.

Now, we were free to reach other villages on Saturdays and Sundays. The weekly trips to the interior continued. So did my sickness.

On entering a village in Sierra Leone, there was a definite protocol to follow. Failure to comply with it could ruin any chance of evangelizing that village. It consisted of going to the village chiefs and asking for a meeting with them.

All of the "big men" of the village would be summoned to attend the meeting. At the meeting small gifts, usually a value less than an American dollar, were given to show respect to the chiefs. Then each chief would formally greet us and with great and elaborate courtesy welcome us to the village. They would ask us to explain our purpose in coming to them. Since these greetings could take considerable time, we had to be patient in letting local custom take its full course. Since every word passed through an interpreter, the time involved could extend for hours.

At last, we could speak. We responded with the same elaborate courtesy and respect that they used when addressing us. We explained that we came to bring the Word of the one true and living God to the village. We came to help and not hurt, to bless and not curse, to teach truth, and we requested permission to minister in their village.

When we finished talking, they would often respond with questions about practical benefits they hoped we would supply to their village. "Will you build a school for us? Will you bring us a clinic?"

It was very important at this point to be clear about our intentions. There could be no ambiguity. There could be no statements that they could construe as a promise of any benefits other than spiritual ones. The slightest hint of a benefit would be taken as a solemn promise.

Almost invariably we received permission to conduct our services. We also received the cooperation of nearly every person in the village. The proverbial red carpet was rolled out, and we were treated as honored dignitaries. Their best food was prepared. The chief sometimes vacated his home so that we could occupy it. Word was sent throughout the village of our coming and our purpose. Everyone was aware of our presence. All of our party and all we possessed was protected by the chief and, therefore, by all his people.

When our service would start in the evening, the people would come from everywhere—from their farms, their markets, and their homes. Sometimes every person in the village would be there. Many would stand throughout the entire service. If it rained, they would stand in the rain. Usually there were no benches, or not enough benches, so the people had to stand.

At the close of the service, the altars were always full.

We needed no pleading altar calls. They responded readily to the gospel and came to receive the spiritual benefits the Word of God offers.

When it was time to leave the village, they brought gifts. Sometimes it was rice or fruit, but sometimes they gave us a live chicken. We were accepted. They wanted us to come back again.

SIX

I N LATE 1976 WE WERE introduced to another young man, a Sierra Leonean named Anthony Juana. Brother Juana had come to the Lord in Liberia under the ministry of Brother Joseph Yarkpai, the pastor of Fassama Mission Station. He wanted to return to his own country and work with us, and he came well recommended by Brother Yarkpai.

Brother Juana proved to be very bold and aggressive in getting things done. He was of the Mende tribe from Gbado, a large and relatively prosperous village.

Gbado was located in a part of the country that had diamond mines. Most of the village men made their living searching for diamonds. Nevertheless, it could only be classed as desperately poor by any American standard. The homes were of mud block or mud stick construction with either a thatch or corrugated tin roof. Usually the floors were dirt and any furniture was rough and sparse. Mattresses consisted of a grass-stuffed tick that was hard and scratchy and that harbored bedbugs. There was no electricity or plumbing.

Brother Juana had a real impact on Gbado. Services were started, and soon a large piece of land was donated for a church. The new members cleared the land, which was a major undertaking inasmuch as it was covered with jungle. Then they set fire to it to burn off all the trees and brush that they had cut down. Unfortunately, they lost control of the fire and had to stay up the entire night to prevent it from burning the village down.

Soon construction began on a new church building. The foundation was laid and the blocks for the walls prepared.

In the meantime, Brother Juana was reaching out to the surrounding villages, preaching everywhere he could. Several young men followed him in his evangelistic tours. He began services in Palima, Gangama, Taninihun, Lavuma, Geneh, Borborbu, and a couple other villages. In each of these villages the response was wonderful.

It soon became evident that doors were opening faster than we could go through them. We were able to start churches, but we did not have pastors to look after those churches. We needed trained men, trained pastors, and we needed them as quickly as possible if we were going to grow.

We did the only thing we could do. To meet the pressing need we developed a six-month crash training program to provide pastors with sufficient training to minister to their people.

We set up four beds in our garage to accommodate our first students. Three of them came through the ministry of Brother Juana. The four students were Anthony Gossimo, David Sesay, Felix Abdullai, and Egerton Jones.

These students went to church every night for six months, and often they went in the daytime or passed out tracts or visited people. They studied Monday through Friday and had tests every Friday. Fifteen years later three of these men are still in the ministry, and two of them are members of the National Board.

Training these men was an unforgettable experience.

Three of them were straight out of the bush and had never seen the most rudimentary inventions of modern times. They had good minds but were totally unexposed to things we take for granted.

When the students came, I showed them where they would sleep and eat and where the bathroom was located. The bathroom was attached to their sleeping quarters and contained modern plumbing. I assumed they understood the operation of a modern toilet, which was a mistake. These men had never seen a toilet that consisted of more than a hole in the ground. We were shocked to find out that they were standing on the commode and using it like a pit toilet. When the commode got full, they did not know what to do next, so I explained in detail about the operation of this modern device. They were mightily impressed by this miracle of technology and thereafter flushed the commode as often as they could, even if nothing was in it.

On one occasion, one of the students had a telephone call. I called him to the phone, but he had never seen one and did not know what to do with it. He was actually so terrified at the idea of using the telephone that his whole body trembled. He held the phone the full length of his arm away from him upside down and yelled at the instrument. Of course, he could not hear anything holding the phone like that. He feared that telephone as if it had been a snake. Finally, we calmed him down enough to get his message.

On another occasion, another student with a wonderful sense of humor was in our home. As he was leaving, he saw his face in a mirror across the room. He turned to another man who was standing nearby and asked, "Who is that man?" He had never seen a mirror before. He had never seen his own face before.

The students asked Sister O'Keefe why she never

washed clothes. (They had never seen her beating them on the rocks or spreading them on the bushes to dry.) She proved that she did wash clothes by showing them our washing machine and dryer. Their comment: "The white man is too clever."

They wondered how Sister O'Keefe baked bread because they saw no big outdoor oven. So she showed them a modern stove with an oven in it. These things boggled their minds.

We had a lot of fun laughing at and with these students. Their sense of humor was great, and they laughed as much as we did.

We played many tricks on them, all in good fun. For instance, Sister O'Keefe chased one student around the house with a vacuum cleaner, putting the suction hose on him whenever she could. He yelled and ran to escape.

Someone told the students that the sound of shoes clattering in the rotating clothes dryer drum was actually a fire upstairs and they had to evacuate immediately. Frantically, they grabbed everything they owned and threw it over the compound fence, while my sons practically rolled on the ground laughing at them.

My sons declared that they could show them magic. The students watched in awe as my boys turned one of the knobs on our stove. In a second, fire blossomed, to the amazement of the students. Later we explained how the fire came.

These men were being exposed to a strange new world. They had never seen water come out of a pipe. They had never been out of their little village area in the bush. They had never been to their own capital city or been exposed to the congestion, rush, traffic, and pressure of a city.

As was to be expected, differences arose among the students. Three of the men were from the bush, but one of them was a city boy and used to a different lifestyle.

Soon it was the season for the termites to swarm again. The men from the bush considered these creatures a delicacy, so they filled a large pan with water and placed it under the light bulb in their quarters. When the termites swarmed to the light, they fell into the water and could not get out. On a good night the students could collect quite a few like this. The termites could be eaten raw, or cooked and eaten like popcorn, or mixed in rice to add flavor and protein.

Our city boy did not want any bugs in his rice. While the other students were gone he threw away the contents of the pan. When they found out what he had done, things got hot. I had to go down to their quarters to cool tempers and mediate the matter.

I have to admit that I could understand the city boy's point of view. I have never been able to muster the courage to eat termites.

In the meantime, our Sierra Leonean friend who had accompanied us from Liberia went to Songo to hold some services. While he was there he heard about another village just two miles away called Gerehun. He walked the trail to Gerehun and there met Samuel Fofanah, who declared that he was the pastor of a small group meeting there. Our minister told him about our one God, Jesus Name baptism, and the baptism of the Holy Ghost, with the result that the man wanted to know more, and he wanted to meet the missionary.

An appointment was made. When I got to Gerehun, a little group of twelve to fifteen were sitting in a semicircle in front of the pastor's broken-down mud house. Samuel Fofanah was tall and skinny and had a high-pitched voice that did not seem to belong to his body. He and his people were ragged and the poorest of poor.

I was thrilled when Brother Fofanah told us that he

had been reading his Bible and saw that baptism in Jesus' name was the scriptural manner to baptize people. He had already baptized all his people in the name of Jesus, but none of them had received the Holy Ghost.

The service started. The people sang and clapped their hands. When it was time for me to speak, I told them about the new birth. They wanted it.

When the preaching was over, one after another they began to speak in tongues as they were filled with the Spirit of God. They all received this experience. I could not help but think of Acts 19:1-6, where Paul met twelve men at Ephesus and asked them, "Have ye received the Holy Ghost since ye believed?" This was worth shouting about.

In conducting our training program, we realized that Sierra Leone has a serious problem with illiteracy. Only about ten percent of the people can read and write.

The teachers are inadequately trained. Many of them have only an inferior tenth-grade education. The students usually do not have any textbooks, because their parents do not have the money to buy them. A full set of second-hand paperback textbooks would cost the average man the equivalent of a couple of months' wages. Consequently, a school may have only a single textbook and sometimes no textbooks at all. When people do become literate, there is such a famine of reading material that many revert to illiteracy.

There are no free, tax-supported schools. Students must buy their uniforms, pay full tuition, buy any supplies or textbooks, and in some cases supply their own desk and chair. Of course, many of the children never attend one day of school, and many of those who do attend never become literate.

All the textbooks are in English, which most of the children do not understand, but their own tribal dialects have never been reduced to a written language or else there is an extremely limited amount of literature in their language. Consequently, if they are literate at all, they are literate in English. The only people who are literate in their tribal languages are literate in English.

The result is that a tract ministry has a limited value. Most people cannot read the Bible in English, and if it were translated into their language they still could not read it. Therefore, the church depends on a verbal gospel to evangelize, teach, train, and pastor most people.

This situation made it necessary for us to require that all Bible college students be able to read and write English. All our many training and teaching texts were in English, and there was no practical reason to translate them into the tribal languages. Since there was such a variety of languages, the only alternative was English.

It seems strange, but groups of Bible translators give many years of their life to learn a new language and then translate the Bible into that language, only to have a finished product that nobody is able to read, with the possible exception of a few literate souls who already have the ability to read the Bible in English.

At long last, it was graduation time for those in our six-month training program. They were honored with special services and gifts. It was a happy time.

We had invested much in these graduates. We badly needed pastors, so we looked forward to these men filling some of the gaps. Anthony Gossimo went to pastor in Gbado, David Sesay to Palima, Felix Abdullai to Songo, and Egerton Jones, because of his youth, went to Dworzak Farm as assistant pastor.

Felix Abdullai began his ministry with great zeal. Soon he started new churches in Macorbeh and Kissykuyeh.

David Sesay reached out to the villages surrounding

Palima. Most of our pastors were taking care of two or three different churches. Many of them were having church somewhere every night.

Brother Nyanmoh went to the area of Freetown called Temgbeh Town to evangelize. He found a shack with electricity and a light bulb. Right from the first service, the place was packed. After the second service we had a baptismal service for twenty people, almost all of them men.

Brother Nyanmoh was in his early seventies at this time, yet he walked everywhere. He walked from his home to his church at Guy Street. He walked to his new work in Temgbeh Town. When he went on evangelistic tours to the interior, he would walk many miles. He would walk until he was too tired to travel further, rest beside the dirt road until his strength returned, and then continue his journey to a new village that needed the message.

As soon as our first students graduated, we received a new group of students, each of them claiming a call to preach. This group was larger than the first one, so we had to find a bigger and better facility for our Bible college. We rented the upper story of a small house about one block from our house, which made things very convenient.

Among this group of students were Francis Ndaoma, Vandi Mambu, Samba Kallon, Tommy Momoh, Francis Margay, and Peter Smart. Their time of training flew by, and we had yet another much-needed group of pastors.

No matter how fast we trained them, we were never able to turn out ministers fast enough to meet the need. The factor limiting our growth was not our ability to evangelize, but our ability to turn out trained men to pastor the people we evangelized.

Although we were training pastors, evangelizing

everywhere, and baptizing hundreds, we had a problem. Some people were receiving the Holy Ghost, but not nearly the number that should have. People were receiving the message, but they were not praying until they were filled with the Holy Ghost.

I was preaching everything I knew to preach, but still only an occasional man or woman was filled. We prayed ourselves hoarse with people trying to get them to receive the Holy Ghost.

Then an international evangelist, Brother Leo Upton, came to conduct two weeks of evangelistic services for us. Brother Upton was not loud, eloquent, or dynamic, but everywhere he went people received the Holy Ghost. Every service was powerful. In every service people fell on the floor under the power of God.

In fact, so many people were falling on the floor that it became a problem. Those who fell often hindered others from praying and receiving the Holy Ghost. It was comical how we solved the problem. We simply asked people to promise not to fall on the floor when praying. They promised, and they did not fall anymore.

During the two weeks that Brother Upton was with us eighty-two received the Holy Ghost. It was a real breakthrough. And from that time until now, people have been receiving the Spirit of God everywhere, continually. In the last six months of our first term of service, 573 people received the Holy Ghost.

SEVEN

W E HAD A MOTORCYCLE that we kept at the house, and on occasions I would allow my sons to use it. One day Tom and a friend of his took a ride down what we called Peninsula Road. They were riding double and doing all right until they drew near a large group of drunken men staggering down the road led by another drunk man wearing the costume of a country devil. The boys moved to the side of the road to go around them, but the group tried to wave them down to demand money. The boys tried to avoid them and keep going. The man dressed as a devil stepped over to grab the moving motorcycle. The motorcycle struck him and knocked him down, and Tom and his friend went flying through the air. Tom's friend lost a considerable amount of skin. He suffered, but there was no serious wound.

Tom was not as fortunate. He landed on a rock. He got up dazed to face the angry crowd that had caused the accident. The "devil" was not hurt, but he was upset. After some argument the group went on their way and left Tom and his friend to manage their way home.

When they got to the house, Tom explained what had happened. He had trouble talking and his mouth did not feel or look right.

I took him to a dentist for x-rays. His jaw was broken. The dentist set the bone and wired his teeth together, the top jaw to the lower jaw. He had to take his meals through a straw for the next couple of months. Fortunately, we had a blender to liquify his food. He took it well and never complained about the meals or the pain.

Devils play a major part in the beliefs and culture of the Sierra Leoneans. They believe there are bad devils and good devils, playful devils, mischievous devils, and mean devils.

Devils have a part in all of their secret societies, such as the Porro, Bundo, Wunda, Devil Bush, Heart Man, and the many hunting societies. The men dressed as devils always wear the most hideous costume possible, and as they dance down the street, crowds will dance in their wake and throw coins at their feet. Most of these so-called devils and their society followers are very serious about not permitting any photography.

Sometimes runners go in advance of the dancing devils to warn people not to take pictures. On one occasion, I had a visitor from America with me when a devil came dancing down the city street. The runners came and told us to take no pictures, and I told them that we would not. Unfortunately, my visitor chose not to respect their wishes, believing that he could surreptitiously snap a few shots without being caught. He took his shots, but he was seen doing it, and bedlam broke out. The society members wanted to beat us both and destroy our cameras. One man slapped me across the face as the angry mob surrounded us.

Fortunately for us, there was a high officer in the society who was trying to control and calm his people. He told my visitor that he must surrender the film, but my friend pleaded that he be allowed just to give him the last part of the film in order to save previous pictures he had taken. This was agreed upon, and several inches of exposed film were given to them.

We were allowed to go. The situation could have gotten very ugly. I was annoyed at my visitor for violating the promise that I had given to the runners. We could have been seriously beaten, our cameras destroyed, and our car damaged.

When we got back home I was still angry. Then my visitor told me he had not given the society people the frames of film containing the pictures of their devil. After taking these shots, he advanced the frames to the end of the roll. When he had given the film that was at the end of the roll, it had contained nothing. He still had his pictures of their devil.

When he got back to America, he had the negatives developed and printed, and he sent me a copy of the infamous prints. They were worthless. They had been taken at such a distance that figures were essentially unrecognizable. The devil could hardly be seen at all.

Almost everyone in the country belongs to one of the societies, and all of them are founded upon devil worship. The people believe that every member of a society is a devil. The consequences of revealing their secrets can mean death. Those who dance in the devil costumes are considered to be no longer human but literally transformed into devils.

Human sacrifice and cannibalism are still practiced sometimes. When the practitioners acquire a victim, they will cut out the human heart, cut off the palms of the hand and soles of the feet, and cut out the genital area. These parts are offered in sacrifice to the devil. The rest of the body is ritually eaten.

Witchcraft is everywhere in every village. The people resort to witches for fertility, for protection, to talk to the dead, to curse an enemy, to identify a thief, to know the future, for prosperity, for healing of their body, and so on.

There is great faith in the power of witchcraft. It is said that a witch can change himself into a bird and fly through the air, change into a snake, cause fires to ignite spontaneously, walk under water without breathing, make himself bullet proof, put curses on people, heal the sick, and tell the future. On several occasions I have known of European-trained medical doctors referring their patients to a sorcerer for treatment.

There are conflicting statistics relative to the religious makeup of Sierra Leone, none of which are based upon reliable information. In any case, I estimate that the country is seventy percent Muslim. Yet these people are not pure in their observance of Islam. They mix their religion with the local devil worship and animism. Still they observe many of the Muslim beliefs. Fortunately, these people are not dogmatic. They are tolerant and willing to listen to Christianity.

Several aspects of Muslim doctrine have opened doors for us. First, the Muslims believe in one God; they are adamantly opposed to trinitarianism. Second, a true Muslim believes in a moral standard.

Many of them have expressed surprise when I told them that we believe in one God. When I detailed our holiness standards of lifestyle and dress they were favorably impressed.

Religion is an unorthodox mixture in Sierra Leone. Only the saving message of the mighty God in Jesus Christ can meet the needs of the people. He is the only answer.

Annually, the month of Ramadan, as it is called by Muslims, comes around. This is the most important time of the year for Muslims who stay in their own country. Only the pilgrimage to Mecca surpasses Ramadan in importance.

There are thirty days in Ramadan, and from before

sunrise until after sunset each day the Muslims fast. They take no food or drink. They are not even supposed to swallow the saliva in their mouths. Infants and pregnant women are excused from fasting.

After sundown eating is permitted. And they do eat. They eat more food during the Ramadan fast than at any other time of the year.

During Ramadan the Muslims are more careful and faithful to observe the ritualistic liturgy required of them. Five times each day the call to prayer rings from loudspeakers at the top of a minaret at the mosque. Wherever they may be or whatever they are doing, they stop and spread their prayer mats on the ground to pray.

Preparatory to prayer, they are supposed to wash their hands, feet, and mouth. They remove their shoes, and facing Mecca, begin their prayers—prayers that are an empty form, a meaningless ritual; prayers with memorized words that have been numbingly repeated a thousand times.

They pray in four different positions: standing, bowing, kneeling, and prostrate with their heads touching the ground. In each one of these positions, in unison, they recite the prescribed words.

Islam teaches that Arabic is the language of God, so all the prayers must be recited in the Arabic tongue. Because Sierra Leoneans, with few exceptions, do not understand Arabic, they have been forced to memorize foreign words for their prayers. Five times a day they utter their rehearsed words in prayer and do not understand what they are saying.

Several Muslims told us that many of their people believe that Allah, because of the Ramadan fast, will turn his back and not look upon their sins. They take this to mean that they have license to sin for a few days. Thus, while Allah's back is turned, they indulge themselves.

When the thirty days of fasting are over, there is a great celebration. There is a midnight lantern parade with internally lit floats going down the main street. The people have feasts with all their favorite foods. They offer many cows, goats, and sheep as blood sacrifices and then eat their flesh at the feasts. This day is the highlight of the year for Muslims.

The day begins with large gatherings for prayer. Across the country, wherever there is a large open area, hundreds and sometimes thousands gather to be led in prayer by one of their religious leaders. They wear their best clothes as, once again, they pray meaningless prayers to their silent, unresponding Allah.

I have asked them, "When you pray do you ever feel the presence of God? Has God ever touched you? Has He ever answered one of your prayers?" Their answer has always been negative. "No. We have never felt the presence of God or felt His touch. He never answers our prayers."

In witnessing to Muslims in Sierra Leone, I have found them to be open-hearted if you love them. They have many misconceptions about Christianity that need correcting, but I have found them open-minded and ready to listen.

Sierra Leoneans, in general, are not strong believers in Islam, but many are afraid to leave it. There are serious social consequences for those who convert to Christianity. Conversion means being disowned and disinherited by the family, including the extended family. The village and friends of a convert treat him as an outcast, enemy, or dead man. With some families there is a real danger of being poisoned.

In America we have many tax-funded social programs to protect people in hard times, such as welfare, unemployment, disability, Social Security, and Medicare, but none of these programs exist in Sierra Leone. There, the extended family represents the security umbrella. And in a land of intense poverty, this security umbrella is important for survival.

When a Muslim converts to Christianity, he sacrifices that security umbrella. Now, if he or his wife or children die, the family might not even bury their body. Consequently, the church must replace the extended family and the security umbrella.

On many occasions I have preached to groups of Muslims. They have always been polite to me, but some of our preachers have been stoned by them. Yet we have won many Muslims. Some of them are preaching the gospel of Jesus Christ today.

EIGHT

DRIVING, OR BEING driven, in Sierra Leone is unusual for a number of reasons. Since most of the taxi drivers are Muslim they believe the fatalistic doctrine of Islam, namely that all the events of life are predestined and therefore unchangeable and unavoidable. Drivers who are indoctrinated with this teaching feel free to pass on blind curves or over a hilltop confident that an accident cannot happen unless it is destiny, and if it is destiny it cannot be avoided. So they relax and accept whatever fate is theirs, and besides, passing on the blind curve was predestined also. It gets a little scary when the driver is looking at you sitting in the back seat, not looking where he is going at all, while he explains his views on fate. Of course, he will courteously remind you that you have nothing to worry about because he is a professional driver.

When we arrived in the country there were no stop lights. There were some stop signs, but drivers only stopped if they could not go without hitting something.

Several years later we did get about half a dozen stop lights. Again, people went right through the red lights if traffic permitted. With electricity outages and maintenance problems the lights usually were not working anyway.

Especially in the capital, Freetown, I never heard so

much horn honking in my life. Every driver honks his horn. If you are a driver, you are expected to honk your horn. You can be cursed for not honking your horn. In fact, there is a horn language that every driver must learn. The number of honks, the duration of the honk, the intensity of the honk, and the time gap between honks all convey a message. Of course, the expression on the driver's face coupled with other gestures helps you to interpret the horn message. The horn messages say many things, such as, hi, good-bye, see you later, okay, move over, coming through, get out of the way, somebody is sick in the car, hurry up, blankity-blank-blank, same to you, I want attention, go jump in the river, go ahead and pass, I'll wait while you enter traffic, please give me a break, and many other things. A driver might get along without brakes, but he must have a horn.

Some roads and bridges are very narrow, one-car-at-a-time affairs. Near our home was a one-lane bridge crossing a river, and since it was the only road going to the area, it had a fair amount of traffic. Often two vehicles would enter the bridge from opposite directions, which created an impasse that could hold up traffic for hours, because neither driver would give way and back off of the bridge. I've seen a driver turn off his engine, lean back, and go to sleep. Other times I have seen a driver turn off the engine, get out of the car, lock the doors, and walk off, leaving his vehicle blocking passage on the bridge.

At this point, because many other cars are held up, many people get involved in the argument about who should give way. The bridge is filled with people angrily shouting at each other and giving instructions that nobody is listening to. Eventually, the crowd will prevail upon one of the contestants in the battle of stubbornness to give way, but only after he has been convinced that he has won a moral victory. Strangely enough, these confrontations seldom evolve into a fight.

Yet these confrontations are very serious. Many, many people had died at that bridge because nobody would give way to opposing traffic. There were so many accidents on the bridge that the rails were completely knocked off on both sides. Many of the fatalities occurred when one or both vehicles landed in the river below the bridge.

On one occasion, an old man pushing a loaded wheelbarrow got halfway across the bridge when he was confronted by a big city bus going the opposite direction. The owner of the wheelbarrow demanded full rights as a vehicle and refused to give way. Again, the crowd gathered, everybody yelled and argued, but the old man was adamant. He was not going to move. This time the crowd took matters in their own hands. They moved his wheelbarrow to the edge of the bridge where the bus and the other backed-up traffic could squeeze by him. The old man could have done that from the beginning, but he figured he had wheels just like the bus, and he had been first on the bridge. When the crowd moved his wheelbarrow from the center of the lane over to the side, he was angry and indignant at the injustice of it all.

As you can see, we are not without entertainment in our country.

In Sierra Leone trucks are called by the British term "lorries." Lorries are responsible for over half the bad accidents. They are in terrible condition mechanically. Often they have no taillights, headlights, or brakes. And they are tremendous oil burners. They send out a cloud of black smoke that is awesome. Somebody should get a patent on the process and sell it to the U.S. Army as a smokescreen. They must burn about a quart of oil per mile. Little stands selling used motor oil by the pitcher full are stationed along the main road. That is what keeps the lorries going.

These vehicles are continually breaking down. Common problems are a broken rear axle, a ruined rear end, and broken universal joints. When a lorry breaks down, the driver parks right in the driving lane of a two-lane highway. There are no flares, reflectors, or lights to warn others that it is in the road. Sometimes a driver will put green foliage in the road as a symbol that there is danger ahead.

At night it is especially important to be on the lookout for lorries. Most of them have no taillights or even reflectors, and if they do, the dense cloud of black smoke from their exhaust obscures the view of them. Sometimes it obscures the view of the entire vehicle. Thus, it is easy to come suddenly upon a parked, unlighted lorry or a moving, unlighted one.

Probably more dangerous is that many of them do not have headlights either. I have seen people driving down the highway with a flashlight stuck out a window to see where they were going. And sometimes they did not even have a flashlight.

Another problem is the way these vehicles are loaded. The drivers fill the interior and then start stacking things on the roof. I have seen them stacked as high as a two-story house weaving down the road, teetering from side to side, struggling to keep in their lane. Often, the roof carries not only a load of goods but also a load of passengers. Needless to say, in the event of an accident, the roof passengers get scattered far and wide.

And lorries do not care about sufficient clearance when passing another vehicle. They will pass knowing full well that there is insufficient clearance. They expect the other driver to pull over to the shoulder and let them complete this maneuver. Sometimes it is a game of bluff to see who will turn aside and make room for the other. Sometimes neither vehicle gives in to the bluff, and then a terrible accident takes place with many killed. Ninety percent of the time when I took my weekly trips to the interior, I would see a serious accident involving a lorry.

Another common problem is that the drivers never have a driving test. They acquire a driver's license through corrupt means. These drivers work long hours, often 6:00 A.M. until past midnight. Consequently, they fall asleep at the wheel.

The roads are horrendous, and the tires often show thread. Potholes are everywhere. It is impossible to miss them all, and they are deep, dangerous, and jarring.

In the interior, if a pedestrian is struck by a vehicle, the driver will rarely stop, and the culprit is rarely found. Sometimes there is a body lying in the road, obviously the victim of a hit-and-run driver.

Of course, the services of a mechanic are needed from time to time. In Sierra Leone, when a person takes his car to a garage, he must have the service manager serve as a witness as he runs an inventory on the vehicle's equipment. He lists the spare tire, jack, tire iron, wiper blades, horn, battery, and so on. If he does not, the items may not be there when he picks up his car. And not only must he list four tires, he must be specific enough to identify the tires. One driver took his car in for service with four good tires, but when he came back for it, his good tires had been replaced with worn ones. I had my horn taken in one garage.

Mechanics, for the most part, are not particular about parts. They can take something apart, put it back together again, and have parts left over when they are done. They say, "Oh, there were too many parts in there. You didn't need them all." As you can see, Sierra Leone is a challenge, but there is no lack of motivation to pray.

Sierra Leone does have a police force. Really, it does! And it does have laws regulating drivers and vehicles. Unfortunately, the laws are not enforced.

The police do not have any vehicles. They carry no gun nor even a night stick. They have no way to go to the scene of an accident, nor can they chase a law breaker. They are grossly underpaid—about five U.S. dollars per month. Consequently, they supplement their income by setting up road blocks and requiring every commercial vehicle to give them money. If the police recognize a person as new in the country, they will wave him down and accuse him of some infraction of the law: "Do you have a radio in your car? Do you have a license to have that radio? Oh, you do not? You have committed a serious offense. You will have to go to the police station, then you will go to court, and the magistrate will fine you heavily."

First, there is no law requiring a license for an AM/FM radio receiver. The policeman knows that. He also knows that he is not going to arrest the driver or have him fined, but he hopes to scare the person into giving him something to let him go. It is standard operating procedure.

After a person has lived there awhile, the police do not harass him like that. They may stop him, greet him, tell him they are broke, and subtly suggest that a gift be given to them. But the threat is absent, and "no" is accepted if rendered in a friendly manner.

NINE

I WAS SURPRISED ONE afternoon to find three trinitarian pastors at my gate. They were very polite and asked if they could come in and talk with me. I welcomed them into my living room where introductions were made and the proper greetings rendered.

Shortly, they began to question me about the United Pentecostal Church and what we believe. For some time we talked about the oneness of God and baptism in the name of Jesus. I must have sounded rather strong while endeavoring to present an irrefutable case for our Jesus Name message, for they defensively raised their hands to interrupt me. One by one, they admitted that they could not argue against this truth. They said they had seen in their Bibles the verses I had brought to them; they could see the truth. They then asked me if I would please preach this message to their churches. Of course, I agreed. I ended up preaching in ten different trinitarian churches. Some of the services were dynamic.

I preached at one large church with about three hundred in attendance. The pastor was a fine, intelligent man who volunteered to interpret for me as I preached to his Lokko-speaking congregation. I preached on the new birth and felt the power of the Holy Ghost in the message. The pastor was an excellent interpreter, but suddenly he stopped interpreting. I turned to see what had happened. When I did, I saw tears running down his cheeks. Both of his hands were in the air, and he was speaking in tongues: he had just received the Holy Ghost.

We did not have to give an altar call. The people streamed down the aisles to pray. They came until the entire front of the church was filled with people on their knees or lying on the floor, crying out to God. When the altar area and all the front of the church was filled up, others still coming began to fall in the aisles and pray. The Holy Ghost fell, and here and there seekers experienced their personal Pentecost. It was all new to them, but they yielded to the power and conviction drawing them. People were speaking in tongues, crying, and shouting as the Holy Ghost fell on them and filled them.

On another occasion, at a fellowship meeting of a trinitarian Pentecostal church, the place was packed. Various pastors of their organization were present and our wonderful Jesus Name message was preached. The preacher suddenly stopped and asked the pastors if they believed that the Bible taught one God and baptism in the name of Jesus. One by one, those trinitarians raised their hands and acknowledged in front of all the congregation that this was the message of the Bible.

Half of the pastors wanted to join the United Pentecostal Church and a majority of the congregations did, but opposition arose among an older group of pastors and elders who feared they could not carry their present organizational prestige and position with them into a new organization. Some of the church elders did not want to undergo the "indignity" of a new baptism in Jesus' name. Some were afraid that embracing a new doctrine would cause them to lose face with those whom they had erroneously led into trinitarianism. They wanted the message but did not want to pay for it. This group of pastors and elders used their influence to persuade the ruling body of their organization not to join the United Pentecostal Church.

In this they succeeded, but a number of their ministers joined us anyway. It was a thrill to baptize them in the name of Jesus. Seven of them enrolled in our Bible college. Some of our finest preachers came out of those churches.

TEN

MALARIA, BY FAR the greatest killer disease on earth, goes relatively unnoticed in a world that has its spotlight on the AIDS epidemic. Yet AIDS kills only a small fraction of the people that die each year from malaria. AIDS hits the developed world; malaria does not.

Malaria, a mosquito-born scourge, is more than epidemic in Sierra Leone; it is pandemic. Almost everyone in this country gets it sometime or other. It is as common as a head cold is in America.

It manifests itself in different ways. Common symptoms are severe headache, loss of appetite, aches, high fever, chills, and extreme weakness. The cerebral strain of the disease is particularly deadly and requires emergency treatment.

Returning from one of my trips to the interior I knew I was feeling bad, but the onset of the feeling had been gradual and I wrote it off as general exhaustion. We had been in the bush for three days sleeping in the villages and eating their food or doing without food. I needed a bath to get rid of the sticky stench of three days of soaking sweat that had mixed with the dust of the roads and of a dozen villages. I was looking forward to home, seeing my family, sleeping in a real bed, and eating my wife's cooking.

The road was atrocious. It was a pathway of potholes,

thousands of them, and I felt as if I hit every one of them. I felt as if I had been in a fight and lost. The road always gave us a beating. If I swerved to miss a pothole, I would just hit a different one. The five-hour jarring ride home took its physical toll, and it was already midnight. I knew I was tired, but I did not know that I was experiencing the onset of malaria.

We arrived home in the wee hours of the morning to be met by my worried wife. She was as glad to have me back as I was to be back. After we unloaded the van, I got my bath and made it to bed, but before the sun came up, I knew I was sick, very sick.

As the fever raged, I kicked off every covering. Then the chills came and I froze. My whole body shivered and shook violently, uncontrollably, as I sought every covering I could get. Then the fever ravaged me again. Then the chills. Then the fever. Then the chills. Then the fever. I dreaded the chills, but the fever was fearful, because I felt it was the most dangerous and damaging.

We did not know immediately what was wrong. Consequently, the disease got a good grip on me by the time we diagnosed malaria. We prayed and used the medication indicated. After three days the fever broke. I was as weak as a burnt reed. I still could not eat. In five days I had lost about twenty pounds. Even though the fever had broken, I was still a sick boy. I needed rest, and to get up too soon would have been risking a relapse.

I was lying in bed on the fifth day of sickness when a young man, about twenty-six, who had been visiting us from America came running to the house with a problem. He had been down by the beach with my son Tom when they spotted a large fishing canoe high up the shore above the waterline. It was large and very heavy. Nevertheless, they decided to launch it and have some fun with it.

It was too heavy for just the two of them to slide directly in reverse to the water. They laboriously turned it sideways and then turned it over and over to get it near the water.

At some point, some friends of the owners of the boat saw what was happening and called them. When the owner showed up they were outraged. The boat was a commercial fishing boat considered to be of appreciable value by local standards. The young man and my sixteen-year-old son had criminal charges brought against them for attempted theft and malicious vandalism. The police were brought in, and arrests were considered.

At this point, my visitor, Tom, the boat owners, and the police showed up at my front door. I shakily got out of bed and got dressed. I did not need any problems, feeling the way I was, but problems do not come at our convenience. I went downstairs, sat down, and let them unload the problem on me.

The boat owners claimed that their boat was damaged. I offered to have it repaired by a qualified marine carpenter, but they refused. They wanted a new boat. I refused. On investigation, the boat proved to be old, in a bad state of repair prior to the incident, and in addition, it had been legally cited as a dangerous craft, having caused a drowning death only a week earlier. The canoe had not been in use because it was legally barred from further use.

Nevertheless, we were in the wrong, and I needed to see that the owners were compensated. However, I did not want them to take advantage of the situation in order to get excessive compensation.

Sick or not, I had to go to the police station. Fortunately, the chief of police was a fair man who realized that theft had not been a motive, and although damage had been done, it was through ignorance rather than any malicious intent. Thankfully, criminal charges were dismissed and we were free to go. I went home and went back to bed.

Of course, the boat owners were free to bring a civil suit against us, and they did. About this time my visitor returned to America, and since my son was a minor I was the only one sued.

I continued to offer more than fair compensation for the boat and went out of my way to be polite and friendly to the owners. It must have helped, because just after the beginning of proceedings they dropped the case and I never heard from them again.

My visitor of those days is now older and wiser, and we have in more recent years been able to laugh about the whole incident, but at the time it was not funny. I would have been tempted to plant my foot in the seat of knowledge if I had not been so weak at the time. Just kidding!

ELEVEN

THE PEUGEOT 504 station wagon that we were driving was a well-engineered car and gave us good service. We had put about one hundred thousand miles on it, but the motor seemed as good as new. The suspension was another matter. It had taken a terrible beating from the rough roads, so we had a considerable conglomeration of rattles, squeaks, and groans continually assaulting our ears. In two and a half years I had gone through seven sets of shock absorbers.

These roads were rough on tires, too. On one of my trips to the interior, my two younger sons, Tom and Don, went with me. Things went well until we started back toward home. Then flop, flop, flop! The tire was flat. I got out, jacked up the car, and put the spare on. We jumped back in the car and started toward home again. I got about two miles further along and flop, flop, flop, flop! Another flat tire! I did not have a spare now! What's more, I had reached a point exactly midway between the only two towns that possessed any services to help a motorist. I was more than twenty miles from help in either direction.

I didn't cry. I did not mention anything about Murphy's Law either. Even though it seemed that somebody was picking on me, I did not blame anyone. And it was raining, raining hard. With a certain amount of disgust, I set about to rectify our problem. There was nothing to do but get out and get the job done. I got out on the wet road, got the jack under the car, and took the second flat tire off the car.

I had to decide which flat tire to get repaired. I made a choice, then with tire in hand, I flagged down the first poda-poda that passed. My tire was thrown on the roof, and I squeezed into the back with a host of other travelers, and I do mean squeezed. I don't know how they got me in there.

I left Tom and Don with the car to guard it while I traveled about twenty-five miles back the way I had come. Thankfully, there was a gas station, it was open, and yes, they could repair a flat tire. Wonderful!

The repairman claimed that he found fourteen holes in the tube. He did not have enough patches, so he cut the patches he did have into halves and quarters to cover the holes. Finally, all the holes were patched, air was in the tube, the tube was in the tire, and I was ready to go.

The man charged me for each hole as if it were a separate flat tire. He took most of my money just to fix that one tire. The repairman was quite plain about his charges. He said, "It is raining, and you have to have my help. So I can charge you high and you must pay." I couldn't argue with that kind of reasoning, so I paid.

Anyway, I was glad it was done. I caught a ride on another poda-poda going back to the car. By now, it was dark out. It had taken about four hours to get that tire fixed.

The boys were glad at long last to see me back with the repaired tire. We would get it mounted and be on our way again.

It was still raining, but I got the tire bolted down. We threw the jack, tire iron, and ourselves into the car. We were dirty and tired but relieved to be going again.

In less than two miles, the tube with fourteen expensively repaired holes in it went flat again. I do not have a persecution complex, but it was now obvious that there was a conspiracy against us.

Going back to the highway robber repairman was out of the question. I took the other flat tire, and standing in the rainy night, flagged down my third poda-poda of the day and headed towards the town that lay in the direction of home.

I waved good-bye to Tom and Don again. I knew they had to be tired, but there was nothing I could do but what I was doing. It was late when I reached the town of Masiaka. God taking mercy on me, I caught the only mechanic in town just getting ready to go home. He fixed the tire and tube for a reasonable charge, which left me enough money to get another poda-poda back to the car.

I got the tire on the car, and once again we were ready to go. Still, we had no spare tire. Would we have another flat tire? We still had over seventy miles to go. I prayed for all seventy of those miles.

We got home in the wee hours of the morning. I was dirty, greasy, and tired.

Tom and Don were beat, but I really appreciated how well they took the weary waiting and long miles. They were good companions.

Some days later, Abbie and I left the house about 10:00 A.M. to tend to some business in Kline Town, an area in Freetown. We were gone until about 5:00 P.M. dealing with some customs matter. When we tried to return home, we were shocked to find that a riot had broken out in town. The streets were barricaded. Shots were being fired. All stores and shops were closed and barred. Mobs were milling about.

We had to get home! Our three sons were there. We did not know how widespread the riot was, and we did not know if the neighborhood where we lived was affected.

A policeman approached us with a rifle and told us he would take us through the riot. Abbie, I, and the policeman got in the car and took off. He told me to drive as fast as I could and to stop for nothing. I went around barricades and through barricades. Bullets were flying all around us. The streets were filled with trash and debris.

If anybody got in our way the policeman threatened to shoot them on the spot. He so frightened the driver of another vehicle that the driver and all the passengers jumped out of the still moving car and let it continue down the road unattended until it crashed into a roadside kiosk. Abbie was crying and praying for God to spare our lives, while I drove and while the policeman tried to console her between the death threats he was shouting out the car window.

At the speed I was going, it did not take long to reach the Central Police Station. I was instructed to stop at the station. Our escort had to leave us at this point, but he told us to get another escort from inside the station. I went in, approached the police chief, told him my story, and asked for a police escort to get my wife and me home.

He said, "You don't want a police escort. Everybody is mad at the police. That is what the riot is all about. You will be safer without a policeman in your car."

He was right. We saw no more barricades, for we had already passed through the worst area. We were able to proceed to our home without further problem.

Still, that riot had been nasty. Over fifty people were killed and many more injured.

Sierra Leonean hospitals and medical facilities are incredibly wretched and miserable. At the main government hospital, wounded people from the riot were everywhere. They were lying on the floor or two to a single bed, and blood was on the floors.

The floors looked as if they were rarely washed. The glass was broken out of most of the windows, and mosquitoes passed through them unhindered. Most of the mattresses had huge holes completely through them. The patients had to situate their bodies in such a way as to avoid the holes. Everywhere there was the all-pervasive reek of stale urine and sweat. The hospital had no sheets, blankets, pillows, towels, or soap. If patients wanted those things they had to bring them from home.

There were bathrooms for the ambulatory patients, but they were dirty and they stank, because the plumbing had stopped up long ago. Some patients, being incontinent, lay in their bed fouled by their own body wastes. Sometimes they were cleaned, and sometimes they were not.

No medicine was provided. The family or friends of a patient had to go to the various pharmacies in town to locate all needed supplies, including blood, plasma, needles, syringes, drugs, and bandages. After they purchased these supplies and delivered them to the patient, he had to be very careful to safeguard them against theft.

Commonly, the x-ray machine would not work because there was no electricity. When the electricity went off, as it frequently did, it went off without regard to area or circumstances. Sometimes the power outages happened during surgery, leading to tragic results.

The facilities were poor because of the extreme poverty, yet I want to give credit where it is due. Sierra Leonean doctors were trained in developed countries, mostly in Europe. They faced the horrendous task of providing care where medicine was either inadequate or unavailable, technology was scarce, trained technicians were few, laboratory equipment and services were almost nonexistent, surgical tools were rare, there was no ability to maintain sterile equipment, and the government paid them about twenty dollars per month for their services. In spite of these obstacles, the doctors adapted themselves to the reality of their situation. They improvised. They used the tools at hand. They diagnosed by experience and treated patients to the best of their ability, and they did a good job considering the daunting task that faced them.

Sister Glenna Jones started attending our ministerial training classes at night. Her sincerity and sober dedication were evident from the start.

She came from an exceptional background and a notable family. Her father was a doctor; one sister, two brothers, her son-in-law, and her niece were all doctors. Another sister was the principal of a high school. One brother-in-law was a doctor of law who once taught at Harvard and later served as Sierra Leone's ambassador to the United Nations. He also served briefly as the chief justice of the Supreme Court. Another brother-in-law was a member of the president's cabinet, serving as minister of Labor, Energy, and Power. A sister-in-law was the head of the National Museum Society.

Sister Jones herself spent twenty years in England working as a nurse. When she returned to Sierra Leone, she became the head matron for the Leprosy/Tuberculosis Hospital located about five miles from our home. In spite of the advantages that her family had been able to give her, she was a humble woman who wanted nothing more in life than to be a faithful servant of Jesus Christ.

After her first year of Bible college, she transferred from our night college to day classes. After two more years of study she graduated and immediately applied herself to spreading the gospel. She held services in the hospitals, on the streets, in her home, wherever she could.

In time, she became our national Ladies Auxiliary president. Although she was about sixty years old, she would walk many, many miles to preach. She helped organize and motivate the women of the United Pentecostal Church into a constructive, cohesive unit.

She never asked to be reimbursed for the many expenses incurred in the promotion of the Ladies Auxiliary, even if her trips took her far into the interior. She spent her nights ministering to the poor and uneducated, always longing to lift them up and strengthen them in Christ.

Her mother was a sweet woman, eighty-nine years old. She was quite heavy and bedfast most of the time. She always wanted us to pray with her and for her.

It was a good day when we filled her bathtub almost to the brim and immersed Mama Cummings in the name of Jesus for the remission of a lifetime of sin. Thank God we did, because she died not long after her baptism.

Sister Glenna Jones is continuing on for God, always praying, fasting, and ministering.

TWELVE

A T THE END of 1991, the United Nations published a paper listing the countries of the world in order of development. Sierra Leone was last. It was named the least-developed country in the entire world.

The study had taken into consideration such factors as annual per capita income, available medical facilities, status of infrastructure, general standard of living, educational levels, overall literacy, life expectancy, infant mortality, and so on. What a sad distinction to be named the least-developed country on earth!

Even more tragic, the country had the natural resources to do far better. In fact, it was rich in mineral wealth. Diamonds, gold, iron ore, bauxite, and hardwood were in abundance, but that abundance went into the pockets of a few grossly and blatantly corrupt government officials and businessmen. These few possessed wealth on a level that was disgraceful considering that surrounding them were the masses of the poorest country on earth and that they had stolen their wealth from the desperately poor.

It is a horrible fact of sociology that children suffer first and worst in conditions of extreme poverty. It was so in Sierra Leone.

The infant mortality rate was unbelievable. Fully fifty percent, one half, of all babies born there died by their second birthday. If they survived the deadly thrusts of malaria, cholera, diphtheria, typhoid, yellow fever, hepatitis, dehydration, dysentery, and contaminated water, they often faced the prospects of serious malnutrition. The signs of malnutrition among the children were so common that nobody noticed the bloated bellies, the reddish brown hair, the sickliness. I have seen cases of rickets so severe that the legs of the afflicted were bent like bows until their little bottoms were only inches from their feet when standing upright.

The children learned to live with hunger, to expect it as a normal part of life. They learned to eat the kola nut, which has no nutritional value but kills hunger. It is a kind of drug that puts nothing in the belly but makes it easier to ignore the pain.

They usually did not know their date of birth, and besides, birthdays were not observed. There were no birthday gifts or Christmas gifts, and toys were unusual and rare. Most little girls would never own a doll, and the dream of little boys was to own a small ball. Shoes were a luxury, and trousers for little boys were unusual.

From the time they were old enough to talk, the children learned to beg: "Master, I am hungry. Please, give me." Most of them never attended school or became literate. Over ninety percent would die illiterate.

They grew up trapped in a cycle of intense poverty from which they could see no escape. Hope was a dead letter soon forgotten, relegated to the realm of useless fantasy. With corrupt leaders as role models, the people soon learned to steal and lie proficiently, but it did not lift them from their pit of hopelessness.

Although Sierra Leone has twenty different languages, not in any of them is there the word "love." The people can say, "I like you," but they cannot say, "I love you" in the fullest sense. Growing up, they never hear a mother or father say, "I love you." There is a void, a gap, an empty place. Life without love is their heritage, the inheritance of a culture depraved by demons.

When the children reached the age of puberty, most of them were put through the initiation rites of devil-based "societies." They were taught to respect devils and accept them as a normal part of life and that great benefits could be derived from catering to them. They were taught to fear and respect witches and sorcerers and to resort to them for special needs.

I have asked them, "What have your devils and societies done for you? You are poor. You suffer. Your country is the last developed of all countries." They knew it was true, but that was their heritage, their inescapable heritage—inescapable until Jesus Christ passed their way. In Him they learned a new word—love. In Him they experienced a new sensation—love.

In Him, hope is born, and the poor and destitute become rich. They are born again to spiritual life, delivered from the living death of hopelessness.

So many times I have seen the lifeless bodies of infants wrapped in a piece of dirty material or a reed mat, carried in somebody's arms to a shallow hole in a weed-covered field to be buried with a brief few words of good-bye. So many times that child died for lack of an available medicine that cost as little as one dollar: too great an expense for an impoverished family. So many times that child died because of malnutrition that left him or her with a weakened immune system unable to cope with the onslaughts of disease. So many times that child died because of a spiritual vacuum that excluded King Jesus, the great physician, the healer of all diseases.

When Jesus said, "Suffer the little children to come unto me, and forbid them not," He reproved His disciples for not allowing children into His presence. When

Jesus spoke those words, surely His view included the children of Sierra Leone. Surely He cares.

His name was Subeh. It was the only name we had for him. He had no mother, father, or known relatives. He lived in a rundown, dirty, derelict building that advertised itself as an orphanage. It was the only home he had ever known.

At age five he had never walked. The medical prognosis was that he never would or could walk. But then Jesus passed by in the form of some Apostolic preachers.

We were conducting regular services in the orphanage, and the response was very good. The parlor was packed with about one hundred adults and children. Subeh always wanted to be in the service, so he was carried and laid down by the front benches.

God always moved wonderfully and powerfully in these services. Many were baptized and filled with the Holy Ghost. One Sunday morning, God took special notice of little Subeh and said, "It is time." The preachers prayed, and Subeh got up and walked all over the church house. He was healed, wonderfully healed, through faith in the name of Jesus Christ.

THIRTEEN

BEING A MISSIONARY in an undeveloped, Third World country does require some sacrifice. Adjustments must be made to a new culture, climate, language, and innumerable other things. There is loneliness, a sense of isolation, vulnerability, and frustration. We miss the American fellowship, the church, the frequent conferences and social events. We miss the familiarity of family, friends, streets, stores, homes, radio, conveniences, and comfort.

But one of the most difficult things that a missionary must do is say good-bye to his children and send them away when they come of age. Mark, my constant companion in travel and evangelism, was eighteen, soon to turn nineteen. The fall semester at Bible college in America was only a few months away. It was time to send Mark back to the United States.

We had mixed feelings about his departure. We were excited for him as he was about to enter a new phase of life, yet we had our anxieties at the thought of him being on his own. Oh, he was not going to be totally on his own. He was going to stay in Pittsburgh, California, at the home of the man who had been my pastor for many years, Brother Jack Edwards. We knew Brother and Sister Edwards would take good care of him, but we also knew that we were his parents, that we were going to be eight thousand miles away from him, that we were not going to be around when he needed to talk to us or needed our help.

There is a time when fledglings must leave the nest, but even when they are out of the nest, parents are close enough to guide them around some of life's pitfalls and occasionally to pull them out of a pit. Sometimes missionary parents feel a sense of guilt, as if they have abandoned their children, leaving them to shift for themselves and to get by the best they can. And sometimes missionary children have a feeling of being abandoned.

We tell ourselves that it is all part of the normal adjustment involved when the apron strings are cut, but there is still a nagging doubt. The question is there: Shouldn't we be with him at this stage in his life?

I prayed much for Mark. I felt a God-given sense of responsibility for him, but I also felt the call of God to be a missionary to Africa. We made every preparation that we could to ensure our son's security and well-being, and then we committed him to the care of a loving and faithful Lord.

Mark was big, strong, good looking, and he had the call of Jesus Christ to preach. When he stepped on the plane to leave Africa, we knew we would not see each other again until our furlough. Now, he did not seem big or strong. He seemed what he was, a teenage boy stepping out of the family nest into an unknown new world that he had to learn to cope with—a world of business, commerce, legal procedures, bureaucracy, taxes, self-support, and responsibility.

We embraced, we wept, we said good-bye, and the plane flew away with our heart.

It was a somber trip home from the airport. Tom, especially, had been close to his brother. They were only twenty months apart in age. Now his companion was gone. Don lost his big brother, Mama lost her baby boy, and I lost my first-born son.

Of course, we missed him. We wrote to him frequently and looked forward to his letters.

But life goes on. Mark got on with his life, and we submerged ourselves in the mission of reaching Sierra Leone.

Even though all our preachers had graduated from our Bible college, it became evident that ongoing training was needed. So we started holding ministers training seminars. They lasted for five days, and we conducted three of these seminars each year.

We brought all our pastors into our Bible college for these seminars. They, together with our students, made up the bulk of the attendance. Often saints from our local churches would also attend.

These seminars were a wonderful source of blessing and strength for our ministers. Some of the most powerful services we had in Sierra Leone took place in our seminars.

These classes and services were so popular that we could not accommodate all who wanted to attend. We finally had to restrict them to preachers and students only.

Word spread about these seminars, and ministers from other church groups asked for and received permission to attend. They came from the Methodist Church, Lutheran Church, Assemblies of God, Limba Pentecostal Church, Lokko Pentecostal Church, and a Nigerian-based Holiness church.

We taught one God, baptism in Jesus' name, the infilling of the Holy Ghost, and holiness. And they listened. Over the years a number of ministers from other organizations came to us for water baptism in the name of Jesus and to receive the Holy Ghost. In the last seminar we conducted during our first term of service in Sierra Leone, just prior to our furlough, two ministers were especially significant. Brother Gobeh was with a Nigerian Holiness church, and Brother Paul Dapaye was with a trinitarian Pentecostal church.

During the seminar they both became convinced of the truth of our message. For a while Brother Dapaye wanted to argue, but when his questions were answered, he and Brother Gobeh submitted to baptism in Jesus' name. It thrilled me to baptize these two trinitarian preachers for the remission of sins.

Brother Dapaye was a unique man in a number of ways. He was an intelligent person, and he was extremely bold in evangelizing. He could seemingly walk into a strange group of people and take over, and the people would listen to him. He was fervently evangelistic. Yet this man was crippled. He could walk, and did walk for many miles to evangelize, but one foot hung loose at the end of his leg. It was useless, as if it were only loosely tied on. It swung different ways, but Brother Dapaye had learned how to get it to land on the ground in roughly the right position by the way he swung his leg around.

Brother Dapaye also had a large, grotesque growth in his mouth that showed when he talked, and it distended his cheek. Yet nothing held him back. This man could preach, and now he was preaching the truth.

One day Brother Dapaye asked to be accepted as a minister in the United Pentecostal Church. He told me he had a congregation of people meeting in a house in a village called Gbendembu, about two miles from my home.

When I went to visit his house church, I was impressed with the people he had. He told them of his conversion and preached the Apostolic message to them.

Without hesitation they received this truth, received the Holy Ghost, and were baptized, all of them, in the name of the Lord Jesus Christ.

Then Brother Dapaye showed me a piece of land that had been given to him for the construction of a church building. He gave this land to the United Pentecostal Church.

Shortly thereafter, construction of a small church started. That handicapped old man worked hard. He carried boards, heavy cement block, and bags of cement. He hauled rock and sand and helped to mix cement manually.

Then one day it was complete: a neat little church that became a revival center for Gbendembu. Many times this little church was filled beyond capacity, beyond standing room, until many had to stand outside, and it pulsated with the power of God.

Later Brother Dapaye became a member of the National Board of the United Pentecostal Church of Sierra Leone.

I decided to give our Bible college students a practical lesson on living by faith. I called them together and explained that they were going out two by two to evangelize. They were going to areas of the country that were unknown to them, and they were going to travel from village to village by foot for one week. They were not to stay more than one night in any village, but they were to preach in each one. They were given no money—none for food, drink, shelter, transportation, or any other purpose. They took no food with them. They were to trust God to supply them with food and a place to sleep.

At first, some were fearful. In fact, two of the students later told me, "Brother O'Keefe, at the beginning of our tour we did not do what you told us to do. We stayed in the same village for two days. We had to sleep on the ground, and we had nothing to eat. We decided that we had better trust God and go from village to village as you told us to do. After that we never did without food again. The people gave us our meals, brought us into their homes, and gave us a place to sleep."

The students all returned glorifying the God who supplied their needs and praising Him for the great response that met their preaching. In that one week, the students started four new churches. About thirty received the Holy Ghost. Later hundreds received the Holy Ghost and were baptized in those churches.

Furlough time was drawing near. We were excited with the thoughts of seeing Mark again, my wife's family, my family, and many friends.

It's funny the things that a person longs for when he is absent from his country. We longed for a real McDonald's hamburger, a genuine hotdog, real lettuce, a fresh peach, a sweet American tomato, strawberries, an American car, and many other things. We wanted to hear American singing and hear some American preaching. We were excited.

But there were mixed feelings. We were considered veteran missionaries now, and it dawned on us that our supporters in the United States would be expecting us to have a veteran missionary's story to tell. It was time to relate what had been accomplished, to give an accounting. That was an intimidating thought. We knew that some good things had happened, but we wondered, Will those who sponsored us be satisfied? Did we do enough? We were working for Jesus Christ, but we also cared about the approval of the many who had given so generously and sacrificially to send us to Sierra Leone.

Though we were excited about our furlough, there were sincere feelings of regret at leaving at all, even for a furlough. I had put my family through a major upheaval of life to come and live here, and we had gone through many things together in adjusting to West Africa and in working to spread the plan of salvation here. I had invested a lot of sweat, tears, sleepless nights, prayers, blood, and messages in the people who were now the United Pentecostal Church of Sierra Leone. They were part of me, and I was part of them.

I had far more sickness than in all the rest of my life. My hair had turned gray. But Jesus was always there at our side. He kept His Word, "Go, . . . and, lo, I am with you alway, even unto the end of the world."

We told our people good-bye and boarded the plane that would bring us first to Europe for our connecting flight and then on to San Francisco, California. As the plane lifted off the runway and gained altitude, I looked down at a scene almost identical to the one I had seen when first arriving in Africa: dirt roads, mud huts, and jungle.

Now I loved those dirt roads, mud huts, and jungle. There I had walked with God. There, He and I had raised up a church.

With my good wife, Abbie, beside me, I looked down at Africa below me and wept.

FOURTEEN

IT WAS EXCITING to see America again. Although we had been traveling for over thirty hours and were exhausted, we were excited. We were back from the war, veterans from the frontlines of battle returning to civilization.

It was so good to see family and friends again after so long a separation. And it was wonderful to see Mark again. Smiles were everywhere as we embraced each one, and tears of happiness flowed freely.

As we left the San Francisco International Airport en route to our pastor's home, I felt strange, even stunned. So much seemed to have changed. Maybe I had just forgotten a lot. Still, there was change. Roads had changed, there were new buildings, some old structures were gone, the lights were different, billboards were not the same, and bridge approaches were altered. I was not as familiar with things as I was before. I felt like a stranger in a new place. It was unsettling to arrive at the place I had known as home for thirty years and feel like a stranger.

I realized that people's lives had continued in our absence and that the wheels of progress ground relentlessly onward. We had been away, absent from the lives of our friends, absent during the progress. Some of them had changed, and unknown to us, we also had changed. Were we to be strangers to these we had known for so many years? Did we have to get reacquainted with our friends?

I had heard that missionaries experienced a culture shock when returning home. I was just beginning to realize what that meant.

The change left me disoriented. I thought it might just be exhaustion and excitement, but as days passed I realized it was more than that.

On the way home we stopped for something to eat at a restaurant. Everything was so nice and clean and orderly. It dawned on me that I was noticing all this because I had missed it, because I had ceased to expect these things. The food, hamburgers and salads, were excellent, it seemed to us. Again, there was the awareness that we had changed.

Still, we were happy and confident. In a few days we expected to readjust to America, to home.

People were extra kind and considerate towards us, and the expressions of affection were many. We were loved, and that was so important.

We were so tired, but of course, we stayed up late talking, grasping at every bit of news of the churches, the saints, fellow ministers, and so on. We did not want to sleep, not yet. We snacked on food we had not seen for years and talked until it was evident that we needed to save some of the talk until the next day.

It was now about 2:00 A.M., and we had been up for about fifty hours. At last, we agreed to go to bed, but as we lay in the darkness a racing multitude of thoughts prevented sleep for some time. Finally, our bodies insisted and shut down the conscious functioning of our mind.

The days that followed were filled with seeing old friends, preaching in the home church, and tending to much pressing business. We quickly acquired a vehicle to use for travel, renewed our driver's licenses, prepared slide presentations, made travel arrangements for numerous obligations, bought some clothes, arranged for our children's ongoing educational needs, and on and on.

Driving in America again required a total readjustment. Everybody drove so fast, over seventy miles per hour, and they came from so many angles. I had not seen a freeway in years, and now I was driving on one. I did not feel confident. The other drivers could tell that I was not reacting as they did. I was too slow, too careful. Seventy miles an hour seemed too fast. Some of them got annoyed with my driving. I realized that I used to drive just as they did and that I would, in time, get used to it again.

As pedestrians, my wife and I had to laugh at ourselves. We felt like bumpkins straight out of the bush. We would hold hands to help each other, look both ways many times, make some sudden decision, start, change our minds, wait, vacillate, decide again, and then with an uncoordinated dash succeed in reaching the other side of the road. It was amazing how much could be forgotten in a few years, even how to cross a street in American traffic.

Still, these were the easy parts of reentry into American culture. The more difficult part soon became evident. We soon realized that we were out of touch mentally with our own country. Thinking, ideas, policies, attitudes, politics, and social concepts had definitely changed. Some changes were not interesting to us and therefore unimportant to us, such as style changes and changes in sports and entertainment stars, but we were shocked and concerned about other changes.

We were shocked by attitude changes that had developed, by the concepts of "assertiveness," by the women's liberation movement, by the liberal sociopolitical philosophies. And people did not seem to be aware that they had changed.

We were also shocked at changes in American society brought about by a new socioeconomic setup. Trade unions had lost power, two-thirds of the women were working on secular jobs, child care centers were everywhere, part-time jobs without benefits were a prevailing policy for many companies, families needed several incomes to cope with the economic pressures, real estate costs were escalating at a phenomenal rate, and medical costs were criminally exorbitant. Economics had affected family lifestyles, and financial pressures forced changes in people's thinking on related matters. Economics affected what people did with their time, where they placed their priorities, and even their value system.

Many people were trying to hold on to the old set of values and priorities but faced constant pressure from the new economic realities. Others had entirely laid aside family values and completely embraced the requirements of present economics.

And we found shocking changes in churches as we traveled across the nation. Some churches that once held a standard of holiness had abandoned discipline. Respect for the ministry, obedience to ministerial authority, and commitment to the church had changed. These foundational principles had been undermined by the liberal elements of society. In many cases liberal viewpoints had infiltrated churches, creating an independent-minded, self-willed laity.

I did notice some favorable changes also. Our churches were bigger, more prosperous, and more missions minded than before. People were wonderfully responsive to the appeal to evangelize the world.

America had changed. Ideas, beliefs, politics, economics—so much had changed. And we had changed. We were no longer on the same wavelength as our homeland. We were out of touch, and it was going to take months of being home to catch up. It was going to take months to get over the culture shock of coming home. This is a strange phenomenon that few of even the kindest and most considerate saints and ministers understand, but it is real, and the longer a missionary serves overseas, the more difficult the readjustment is on each succeeding furlough.

We hit the road, going from church to church, averaging six services a week. I preached until I was hoarse, but the churches treated us wonderfully. There was a great generosity towards missions. We were encouraged by the sacrificial response to our appeal.

We met many, many fine people in our travels. A year passed, our furlough ended, and it was time to say goodbye to family and friends, to America.

Another of our sons, Thomas, had to be left behind as we returned to Africa. We went through the same agony and soul searching in leaving Tom as we did Mark. We tried to meet all his needs, but in the end, we could do no more than put him in the hands of God and keep him continually in our prayers. We loved him as our very life. We worried, but our God is never failing, so we walked on, having committed Tom into the hands of our faithful Lord.

In our deputational services tongues and interpretation brought forth the message on several occasions that God would take care of our children if we would put Him first and serve Him. So we walked by faith.

Our youngest son, Don, was still with us. He missed his brothers, but that was a price he had to pay for my calling and burden.

FIFTEEN

As THE PLANE touched down at Sierra Leone's international airport, the warm, humid air of equatorial Africa met us with its usual oppressive embrace. We gathered our hand luggage from the overhead compartments and made our way toward the exit of the 707. On the tarmac we looked toward the airport building, and there on the second level were many of our pastors waving their welcome to us with big smiles. It was so good to see them. We loved them. They were part of us.

Standing with them were Brother and Sister John Paul Hughes. They had lived in our home during our year-long furlough and carried on the work during our absence. They had done a good job, and we counted ourselves fortunate to have had them serve as our furlough relief.

We got through immigrations and customs in good order and passed into an outer reception area where our welcomers were waiting. Happy greetings flowed back and forth for some time. Then we loaded into our station wagon and headed home.

It was not very far to our house from the airport, but the Sierra Leone River had to be crossed to get there. The river was about five miles wide and there was no bridge. Consequently, a ferry system was the only reasonable alternative. Unfortunately, the ferry system was not always reliable.

It was an interesting and pleasant ride, filled with local color and culture. There was always a mass of women clothed in bright lapas carrying heavy loads on their heads, going to or from an open produce market somewhere. Little handmade wheelbarrows carted loads too heavy to carry. Fishing boats worked the river using patchwork sails for motivation. And there was always a pleasant breeze on the upper deck where we could enjoy the beauty of the view. In one direction we could see miles of delta extending through extensive mangrove swamps. In another direction we could see the skyline of the capital city, Freetown. In yet another direction there was the mouth of the river opening into the seeming infinity of the Atlantic Ocean.

But the ferries were not always reliable. In fact, periods of their history are either infamous or hilarious depending on one's frame of mind.

Some acquaintances of ours had to spend the entire night on this ferry because the engines failed in the middle of the river and there was no radio to call for help. If it had not been for anchors, they would have been washed out to sea.

The ferry schedule and its departures did sometimes coincide, but many, many times they did not. It was not at all uncommon to wait four to six hours for an hourly ferry to arrive. If someone found himself on the wrong side of the river in the evening he might have to wait the entire night for the next crossing. I have seen the ferry bottom out on a low tide and have to sit in place until the next high tide came to the rescue. I have seen it crash into pilings, and I have seen when the currents were so strong and tricky that the pilot could not properly bring it into dock. Two-by-six-inch boards were laid out from the deck of the ferry to the landing ramp whereon brave motorists were expected to drive to reach land. It was spooky, but we made it.

Anyway, we were heading home from the airport with our welcoming committee. We reached the ferry landing at Tagrin Point, bought our tickets, and joined the line waiting to board the ferry. The line was quite long, and it was obvious that the vehicles at the end of the line would not be able to board for this crossing.

Then the word got out that this was going to be the ferry's last run of the day. Pandemonium broke out. Nobody wanted to sleep in a car that night while waiting for the morning ferry. The cars at the end of the line proceeded to drive forward to the front of the line by using the traffic lane set aside for the vehicles that would be coming off of the ferry. Consequently, when the ferry arrived the vehicles that were on it could not get off, and none of us could get on until they did get off.

It was an impasse. The cheaters would not or could not back up. Now that the impasse was a reality nobody seemed to worry about it. All the drivers turned off their engines. Some turned up their radios, and impromptu dances broke out on the pier. Others chatted with friends or went to sleep. Stubbornness set in. Nobody would give. The general reaction to the problem was to feign indifference and acceptance.

It was 4:00 A.M. when the problem was finally resolved. We were blessed to get on the ferry and finally reached home at 6:00 A.M. We all ate breakfast and went to bed around 7:00 A.M.

The revival that had begun during the last year of our first term was still going strong. In fact, it was bigger than before and still growing. We were determined to promote evangelism, so we set up a system where periodically every pastor went on an evangelistic tour. These tours were dynamic. Every service had an outpouring of the Spirit of God. The average week-long revival would have forty people receive the Holy Ghost. Overall, we averaged three people receiving the Holy Ghost in every evangelistic service. The simplicity with which people received the Spirit was amazing. Usually, ten to fifteen minutes of seeking was sufficient.

One of our new college graduates proved to be a natural evangelist. John Samai, as a college student, started four churches. When he graduated he became the pastor of all four simultaneously. He then started a fifth church and pastored it also. He never had a day off. Everywhere he went revival broke out.

Brother Samai was made national evangelist, and other men pastored the churches that he started. He would preach almost every day. Then he started a couple more churches. Literally thousands received the Holy Ghost during his services over a period of years.

Still, this was not a one-man revival. All of our ministers were having a Pentecostal outpouring. After the revival started, there was only one time I was in an evangelistic service where nobody received the Holy Ghost.

The altars were always full. Yet we gave no pleading altar calls. They were not necessary. When the preaching was finished, people flocked to the altars in faith and prayed with a hunger that brought heaven's answer.

Brother Samuel Kolie was only five feet tall. He was skinny, and the clothes he wore were old and ragged. He was the poorest of the poor. He owned nothing but his clothes. He did not even own a pair of shoes, and he was legally blind.

He had a great sense of humor and was liked by all of our people. What is more, he was respected.

Some people ask how he could have studied the Bible if he was legally blind. I know it happened for I was his instructor. God enabled him to read the Bible when his eyesight was so poor that he could not find the door to a house or a car. His eyesight was so poor that he often fell over things or fell down inclines or into ditches. He was legally blind, but he could read the Bible.

He started a number of churches soon after his college graduation. Later he transferred to another region where he raised up a fine congregation in a village called Borborbu. He built a mud-block church building for them and packed the place with people full of the Holy Ghost and baptized in the name of Jesus.

Then he used Borborbu as a base from which he evangelized the surrounding villages. These villages were five and ten miles distant, and he did not own a pair of shoes, but he went anyway. Often he did not have food, and the people he preached to did not have food to give him, so he went hungry, but he went. It was common for him to spend the night sleeping on the ground, a floor or a bench, so that when he would wake in the morning he would be near the people he wanted to preach to. And everywhere he went there was a revival.

Then one day he came to my home very sick. He was diagnosed as having tuberculosis in advanced stages. We prayed, but God did not heal him. Later we found out why. He was admitted to a special hospital and treatment began.

For a while he seemed to respond well to the treatment. He preached in the hospital to other patients, nurses, visitors, workers, and doctors. He preached from his bed, and his room filled with the listeners. Sometimes people stood in the hallway listening when his room filled up. In that hospital there was an outpouring of the Holy Ghost.

Then he got permission to leave the hospital long enough to walk five miles to a village called Lakka. There he preached, and again revival broke out and people received their personal Pentecost.

Then he walked back to the hospital and crawled into his bed. A week or so later he was dead.

He had never married, so he did not have a wife or children. When we buried him not one relative was present. The place where we buried him was just a weed-covered piece of ground, and we did not have an engraved marble stone to put on his grave. In fact, we did not have any marker at all. It is an unmarked grave. If we went back there today, we could not find the place.

But though there was no wife or child to mourn his passing, though there was not one relative to weep when he closed his eyes in death, and though he lies in an unmarked grave, Almighty God knows the place. The angels of heaven know the place. One day a trumpet will sound and the dead in Christ shall rise, and Brother Kolie will be resurrected with an incorruptible, glorified body. He will not be wearing rags anymore, but a royal robe of righteousness, and on his head will be a crown of everlasting life. He will not be blind but will have eyes that behold eternal treasures. He will not walk dusty roads again, but streets of gold.

Men like Brother Samai, Brother Kolie, and many others were God's instruments for revival for Sierra Leone—men who poured themselves out as an offering to Jesus Christ.

There was such an open door, such a responsiveness to the gospel, such an evangelistic response in Sierra Leone that we were never able to train pastors as fast as they were needed to take care of new converts. In an effort to meet this need we expanded our Bible college operation and upgraded the program and the curriculum. We went to a three-year course and made a concentrated effort to recruit ministerial students. We only accepted those who professed a call to preach. Yet the college grew.

We acquired larger facilities to accommodate the growth. The enrollment grew until we had over fifty ministerial students. Not all would succeed, but out of them God was giving us pastors, evangelists, and leaders.

About this time God sent the David Ward family as missionaries to work in Sierra Leone. We were so glad to have them with us. We would have some Christian American fellowship. They readily adjusted to hardship, and Brother Ward was a hard-working, intelligent man with a good education. He took over the complete operation of the Bible college and began to turn out the pastors and evangelists needed if we were to grow and grow strong.

We were also blessed with some Associates In Missions workers who sacrificially gave of themselves to help this work. John Brown was a chemical engineer. He had graduated with high honors from Purdue University but immediately after graduation chose to give a year of his life helping in Sierra Leone. He was highly intelligent, had a good attitude, and was willing to work. He taught twelve Bible college classes every week. In Sierra Leone he felt his call to preach. When he left, he went straight to Texas Bible College to train for the ministry.

PHOTOGRAPHS

Brother O'Keefe preaching on the river bank just before baptizing a group of thirty-five.

Thirty-five were wonderfully buried in the name of Jesus Christ in the above scene.

Ten were baptized in the waters of the Atlantic Ocean.

A scene from an evangelistic outreach on the east side of Freetown. The place was packed. Seekers completely filled the altars.

An altar scene at a General Conference conducted at the Bible college in Goderich. Hundreds crowded the altars.

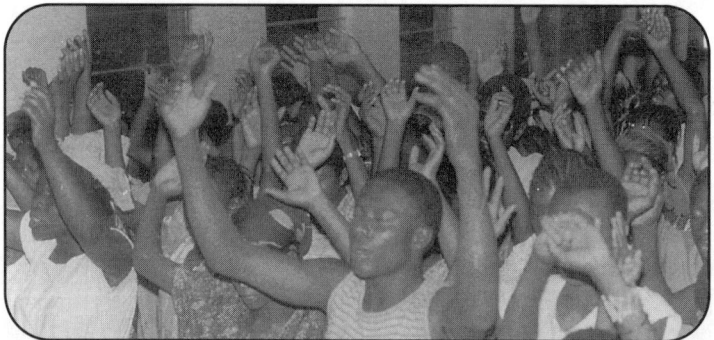

A sectional conference at Juba produced eighty-two infillings of the Holy Ghost in three days.

A trinitarian pastor went down in the water in Jesus' name.

His entire congregation followed him into the waters of baptism.

A total of twenty adults received the Holy Ghost and were baptized immediately afterwards in this night scene.

Here is the other half of the above scene.

In one year over two thousand received the Holy Ghost. One to two hundred received the Spirit every month.

The response of the hungry was awesome. Most of the people were speaking in tongues after just ten to fifteen minutes of prayer.

So many were receiving the Holy Ghost that we were pressed to train pastors fast enough to accommodate the new converts.

Brother John Samai (left) was a great evangelist.   Brother Samuel Kolie (right) was legally blind, but a great man of God.

Brother O'Keefe standing with Brother Nyanmoh.

Little Subeh, five years old, was miraculously healed at a service in the orphanage that was his home.

Brothers Dapaye and Gobeh, both trinitarian preachers, were rebaptized by Brother O'Keefe.

Mud walls with thatch roofs were the common building elements of the village homes.

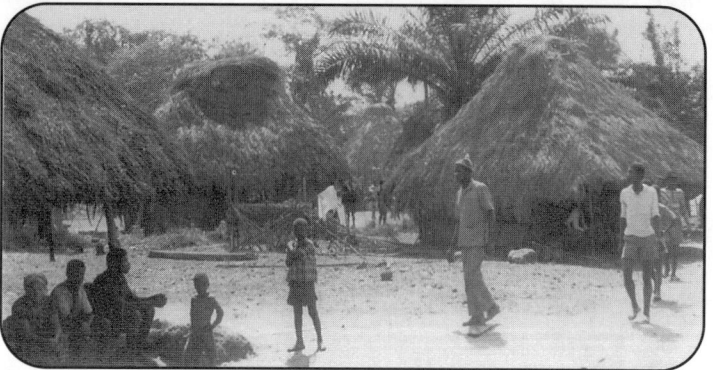

The annual per capita income of the nation was less than two hundred dollars.

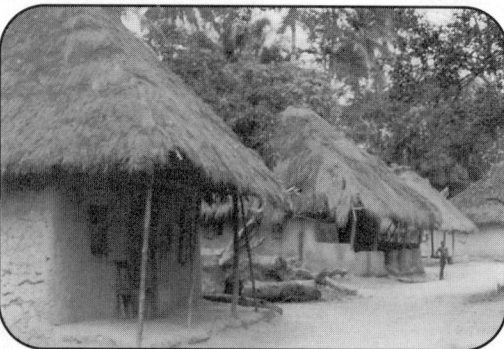

In villages such as these, there was openness and receptivity to the gospel.

Our church in Aberdeen Village was having overflow attendance when soldiers caused its destruction during a military coup.

We traveled tens of thousands of miles on roads like this to reach villages. Some of the villages could only be reached by footpaths that went deep into the bush.

This path leads into Gbado, a large village that nearly burned down while we cleared the land for construction of a church.

Seventy percent of Sierra Leone is Muslim and mosques fill the land. They are in every village.

This group of Muslims stood in the rain to pray a ritualistic prayer to Allah in a language they did not understand.

They bowed their heads to the ground as they followed their imam (leader) in the prescribed movements and words of their ritual.

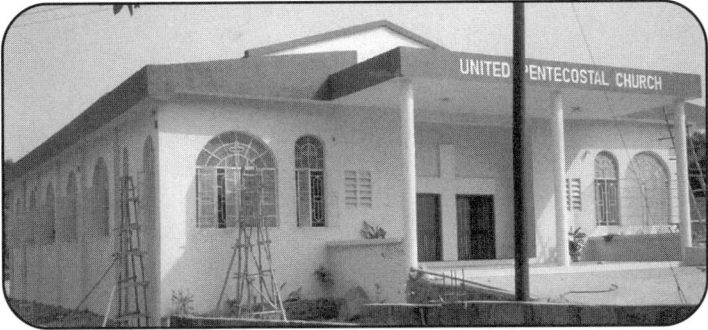

Our new headquarters church and offices were completed in early 1993. It can seat 900, but with people standing we can put 1,000 inside.

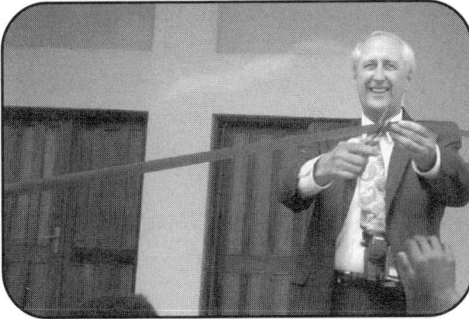

February 6, 1993, was a happy day for Brother O'Keefe when he cut the blue ribbon to open the new church.

The fulfillment of a dream—yes, a vision from God. The church was full. The people wept with an inexpressible gratitude. They danced in the aisles by the hundreds. Victory marches and victory dances were continuous, uplifted hands and surrendered hearts were everywhere, and their faces reflected a sincere and deep appreciation for Christ's sacrificial death at Calvary.

SIXTEEN

OUR YOUNGEST SON, Don, learned to speak Creole like a native. His comprehension was good, and he spoke without accent. He was all boy and liked to do all the things that boys do.

Our other two sons were in America. We had only Don still with us. He was fourteen when we returned to Africa and he meant a lot to us.

Every Saturday morning I would get him out of bed to play basketball at a private court owned by a Lebanese group. Sometimes enough people would show up for an informal game, but occasionally nobody came but Don and me. There were just the two of us the morning he got hurt.

He had grown tall and could get up in the air fairly well, and he wanted to show me that he could dunk the ball. I had seen him do it before, but still he wanted to show me again.

I knew that dunking could get a person hurt if not done carefully, and I was somewhat apprehensive as he started his move toward the basket, but I was never an overprotective parent. I felt that boys must be allowed to do things if they are not to develop into sissies. This was one time I wish I had done differently.

He leaped high into the air with the ball in his right hand and made the dunk, but he did not get his hand away from the basket rim quickly enough. His wrist hung on the rim and his forward momentum carried his lower body forward. When his hand came away from the rim he was almost in a horizontal position in the air. To try to break his fall he threw his left arm back to catch himself as he hit the concrete court. Immediately, both bones in his left forearm broke, a compound fracture. He knew right away what had happened. He called, "Dad, it's broken!"

Our bodies and minds shifted into a crisis mode—a sudden calm coupled with the need to make quick decisions and take emergency action. We needed to immobilize the arm but could find nothing in the area to serve as a proper splint. Finally, a man located a wide, shinglelike piece of material to put the broken arm on. Fortunately, the bone that had come out through the flesh went back into his arm. We were concerned about infection because of the cut, but mainly we felt the need to get the bones set properly, which presented us with the next problem. It was now around noon on Saturday. Very little business took place on Saturday afternoon in Sierra Leone.

We got Don into the car. He held his arm with the shinglelike piece as we drove into town to the doctor's office. The doctor was not there. Don was sitting in the hot car getting sick, yet he was really brave about it. He never panicked, never wept, never complained. He stayed calm throughout his ordeal.

We went from there to another doctor who was just leaving for the day. He was an orthopedic surgeon, and he was prepared to help us. He examined the arm and confirmed the obvious. Still, it was necessary to take x-rays. That was no small matter because there were very few x-ray machines in Sierra Leone, and the few that were there commonly did not work, and if they did work they commonly were shut down for lack of electricity. We located two working machines but had to wait until electricity came on to get the needed pictures. Finally, we got the pictures.

The doctor admitted Don into the best medical hospital in the country, yet it was nowhere near as good as the worst facility in America. Most American veterinary clinics were considerably better than this hospital. Still, I was glad for it. I could not imagine putting my son in the other hospitals.

In Sierra Leone the only people who get medical treatment for a serious need are those financially unable to leave the country to get it elsewhere, but Don's arm needed immediate attention. I did not feel that we could risk flying him to Europe or America with his arm in that condition. We had cause to be concerned about gangrene. A similar injury had caused another boy his age to lose his arm when gangrene set in, and Don was aware of that incident.

The doctor tried to set the bones externally and failed. Surgery was scheduled for the following day but had to be postponed because the only set of surgical instruments was in use elsewhere.

Finally Don was taken into surgery. He was put to sleep by an untrained anesthesiologist who overdosed him, and he did not wake up until late that night. We were deeply concerned about entrusting our son's arm, and even his life, to unqualified personnel, but we felt that we had no alternative.

When he came out from under the anesthesia he was quite groggy for some time. Gradually he recovered from the overdose.

Stainless steel plates had been screwed onto his broken bones to fasten them. No cast was applied when he was released from the hospital a few days later. He was told that a cast would be unnecessary, but as the days passed Don felt that the bones were moving in his arm. Further x-rays confirmed that they had indeed moved. The doctor who x-rayed him this time privately warned us that we should get back to America for correction.

Don also noticed that he had lost feeling and movement in parts of his hand. We thought it would come back in a few days or weeks, but we saw no change.

It was evident that Don was going to have to go to America for another operation. We sent him ahead of us, but the American doctors refused to touch him unless his parents were present to sign waivers. We flew in and completed the arrangements.

After examining the work done on Don's arm, the American doctor said something that I never thought I would hear a doctor say. He said, "I would suggest that you sue the doctor who did this operation." Of course, that was impossible in Sierra Leone, and we never considered it.

New surgery was performed, which involved new steel plates and bone grafts, but Don never has recovered full use of his arm. He has limited forearm rotation and loss of use of his index finger due to nerve damage and atrophy of muscle tissue. He has grown used to his handicap and now works on hard physical jobs.

Throughout all of this we were continually in prayer, seeking God to help us. He did. We do not understand everything in God's plan, and we do not know all the reasons, but we love and trust Him. Sometimes He uses heartache and pain to mold and shape us, to form in us the spiritual assets necessary for growth. We can do nothing else but trust Him, for He is worthy.

SEVENTEEN

OUR ALTARS WERE invariably full of seekers. And our time at the altars was always exciting, crowded, spiritual, and extremely hot and humid.

We did not give altar calls. There was no pleading or begging for a response to a message, nor were there any special music or songs designed to draw sinners to their knees. Those things were not needed. Unbidden, the people flocked to the altars as soon as the preaching was over.

So often the seekers were so tightly packed at the altars that it was difficult for us to reach some of them to pray with them. The closeness of crowded groups praying fervently generated a lot of heat, which added to a heat that was already almost intolerable. The sweat ran from the seekers until their clothing was soaked, and we who prayed with them also became soaked with sweat, both theirs and ours. The altar work was just that, work. It left us feeling sapped of strength, washed out, drained, exhausted. Yet the thrill of seeing and hearing seekers filled with the Holy Ghost was more than adequate compensation. Service after service we were rewarded with the cry of newborn spiritual babies speaking in tongues that they had never learned.

Our National Conference was to take place in a bush village called Songo. The chiefs allotted a piece of ground for our use, and we began construction of a palm-branch shelter. We cut and trimmed bush sticks for posts to hold up the roof, cut palm branches to provide a roof for shade, used bark strips and vines to tie it all together, cut bamboo to form rails and benches, and gathered stones to make a platform. After weeks of work we had our conference hall. It had a dirt floor and open sides, and the benches were backless. We strung wire and hooked up a little portable generator to give us lights for the night services, and we brought in our battery-operated speaker system.

Since Sierra Leonean villages do not have motels, hotels, or restaurants it was necessary for us to get everyone a place to eat and sleep. We also had to meet the needs of personal hygiene and sanitation. Whenever we conducted a conference all these matters, and others, had to be worked out. It involved considerable planning and organization.

On the first day of the conference people came in by busloads. The people soon settled in and services started. We were packed, and the local village people were excited about the big event. The shelter was full, and the non-Christian local people surrounded it, looking in through the open sides.

Night after night the Holy Ghost fell in a powerful way. The people danced and shouted. Many fell out on the ground. Here and there people were speaking in tongues. The altar area was filled with seekers with uplifted hands and tear-streaked faces. Each night twenty to thirty new people received God's Spirit.

Songo was receiving a revelation of the reality of God. The crowds grew around the shelter as the villagers watched in amazement. Many came in and received their personal Pentecost, yet a very large group had never come inside.

The last night of the conference was the most awesome of all. The saints worshiped with such a demonstration of fervor that they raised a cloud of dust as high as their heads. The crowd of spectators surrounding us saw something that the worshipers did not see. They saw a six-foot cobra crawl into our conference shelter, right into the mass of shouting, dancing saints. They did not tell us about the snake. They did not warn us.

To the villagers, this was a test of our God. They knew that the snake's behavior was unnatural: cobras just do not approach groups of noisy people. There were spirits behind this, and even they could perceive it. The spectators watched to see what would happen.

The Spirit of God was already moving gloriously, but then an even greater shower fell from heaven, and almost everybody in the place began jumping up and down, thrilled and filled with a holy joy. As the people leaped and danced in worship, the cobra was trampled to death beneath the bare and sandaled feet of God's people. The villagers were deeply stirred. Their resistance broke. Many of them received the Holy Ghost, and nearly one hundred were baptized. Most of them had been Muslims.

One young seeker failed to receive the Holy Ghost during the conference, but on a public bus on the way home, his hungry heart opened to receive the flow of living water. Uncaring of his startled fellow passengers, he began to speak in an unknown tongue.

We were in the midst of a move of God, a truly apostolic revival. It was spreading to all our churches, and our pastors and evangelists were reaching out to new villages. Almost all our preachers were pastoring two or three churches at a time. The reports kept coming in. Thirty received the Holy Ghost here, forty-five there, over eighty elsewhere, twenty, fifty, sixty-five, and so on.

The second missionary term was yielding far more

souls than the first. Each month, one to two hundred were receiving the Holy Ghost. By the end of our second term about six thousand had received the new birth.

Every evangelistic service produced new souls. Each week-long revival brought in an average of forty new births.

Physically I was unable to keep up this exhausting pace. We had grown, the administrative load had increased considerably, and I was getting older and weaker as the equatorial climate played havoc with my health. I was wearing down. I knew that we had to make organizational changes if the revival was to continue.

We divided the country into regions and appointed presbyters for each one. We also appointed a national director of evangelism, an assistant superintendent, and other national officers. I began to delegate to our national leaders many of the things I had been doing.

The move proved to be a good one for a number of reasons: it spread out the workload, gave me much-needed relief, increased the manpower devoted to each function, exposed the nationals to organizational duties and taught them leadership principles, freed me to devote myself to new training programs and new administrative needs that evolved with our growth, and helped prepare our people to meet our goal of having an indigenous church.

Brother Nyanmoh became our first assistant superintendent. Our first Sierra Leonean contact became treasurer, and Torboh Johnson was secretary. Several presbyters were appointed as well.

The treasurer, the same young man who had come to Sierra Leone with us from Liberia, was closer to us than any of our other ministers. He lived in a small guest quarters that was part of our home for over five years. He was the first Sierra Leonean we had met, and he had been quite helpful in the early stages of the work. I personally trained him for the ministry, and he was a constant companion in my travels throughout the country. Our entire family had become very attached to him.

He had a good personality, people took to him readily, and he was intelligent. He was an able evangelist, pastor, teacher, trouble-shooter, and organizer. I had heard him at various times do some truly excellent preaching. He also had some faults, some weaknesses, but they had not come to the surface in the early years of our association. His education, natural intelligence, personality, leadership, and general ability coupled together with his close relationship with me made him prominent nationwide as the foremost Sierra Leonean leader in the church.

Towards the end of our second term as missionaries, we were blessed to have another missionary family come to Sierra Leone to serve. Brother and Sister Ramsey with their three children came with a burden for revival. Consequently, he was made the national director of evangelism. He was a powerful preacher and an able teacher. He was intelligent and a good organizer.

They were able to lease a nice home only a block or two from where we lived. We enjoyed a lot of good fellowship with them, and they were a blessing to the work.

Unfortunately, their health was not equal to the hardships. The tropical sun's rays gave Sister Ramsey skin cancers. During their four years in Sierra Leone she had to undergo numerous surgeries, and he suffered with debilitating heart problems. The equatorial climate, the pervasive profusion of diseases, the lack of medical facilities, and the general demands of a poverty-stricken country made continued service there impractical for them. I still remember Sister Ramsey's many tears when the decision was made to leave Sierra Leone.

EIGHTEEN

I T WAS NIGHT and I was two hundred miles in the interior, surrounded by jungle. I had been in the area for a couple of days, preaching from village to village, and I was dirty, sweaty, and tired. I just had a few minor loose ends to tend to and then I would be heading home toward Freetown.

The trip home would be slow, much of it on dirt roads that gave both car and passenger a beating. When we did get to a paved road it was often worse than the dirt roads. There was no way for a driver to avoid the maze of thousands of potholes.

On the way, we stopped at a little kiosk in the middle of nowhere to get a Coke. (Yes, I have found Coca-Cola in the deepest jungle.) As we were drinking our Cokes, a man approached us, coming out of the dark with a box in his hand. In the box was a baby chimpanzee. She was just a little thing unable to stand by herself. The man had killed the baby's mother and wanted to sell me this helpless creature.

I was anxious to be on my way, so I gave the man twenty dollars, put the little chimp in the car, and we were on our way. I had known of other people who had raised a chimpanzee, and I thought my boys would enjoy a new pet.

I reached home about 2:00 A.M. and presented my

wife with the chimp. Abbie did not seem too thrilled about our little ape but resigned herself to help take care of her.

The Mende tribe in Sierra Leone called a chimpanzee *nguli*, which actually means baboon. We decided to name our chimpanzee Nguli.

We fixed up some baby bottles for her and fed her as often as she wanted. She was so little, and at times I wondered if she would survive.

She was very dependent and very affectionate. She wanted to be held constantly and hated to be left alone. To bring her into the house Abbie would put a diaper on her.

After some time she gained strength and became able to walk. Then she started swinging from limb to limb in the trees of our back yard. When she had grown a little, I built a large cage for her in the back yard.

I do not believe in evolution, but Nguli had so many human ways that it was amazing and thought provoking. She had tantrums just like a human child, falling down and screaming, and she would pout terribly. She would cross her arms, stick out her lower lip, and huff and puff. She was curious about everything. She would watch us as we did something and then try to do it herself. If someone was pulling weeds, she would pull weeds— well, mostly weeds, but some flowers also. If someone used a screwdriver, she would want to try it. She was the most intelligent pet I have ever had.

And she was very possessive. She had her baby bottle and her blanket, and they were not just possessions to her, they were security items. She would rock back and forth holding these things. In time we had to wean her from her bottle and blanket. It was an unhappy time for her, but she adjusted.

Nguli had a voracious appetite. She loved bananas more than anything, but she could eat oranges, mangoes, greens, rice, and so on. Her record was forty-two bananas in one day. Fortunately, I could buy bananas for about a penny each at that time.

She was such a good-natured creature that everybody liked her. When visitors came they invariably gravitated to her. We would take her out of her cage, and she would readily go to any stranger who would hold her and give her attention. Everybody wanted to have a picture taken holding her.

If someone was carrying her she would hold on like a leech, with both hands and feet. And as she grew she became increasingly strong, yet she never hurt anyone. We could carry her on a hip or put her on our backs, and she would hold on and never tire. Or we could put her on the ground, take her hand, and walk with her, but if we put her down and acted as if we were going to leave her we would hear her screams from a distance.

She could not talk, of course, but she did make a variety of sounds, and it was easy to know which emotion she was expressing. She always greeted me with an ooh-ooh-ooh when I got home, but other ooh-ooh-oohs were obviously complaints.

She was good-natured about most things, but she hated to be bathed. She would carry on terribly about soap and water, screaming as if she were being killed. When the ordeal was over and she was dry and brushed, she was a fine-looking little chimp.

And she hated the veterinarian. He had given her injections and used a rectal thermometer on her. Nguli was highly indignant about the thermometer, and when it was removed she turned and cursed that veterinarian terribly in chimpanzee language. She never forgot and never forgave. Every time she saw him after that she gave him a new cursing.

Chimps live to be about thirty-five years old, and it

takes them about eleven years to reach full maturity. A full-grown male can weigh up to 180 pounds and can lift 600 pounds. Their strength is far greater than most people realize.

In spite of Nguli's strength, she could be exceedingly gentle. We brought a little puppy named Pierre to her once, and she immediately recognized it as a baby. She was so gentle with the pup that it was a touching sight; she petted it with the lightest caresses. She was as instinctively gentle and careful as a human being would be with a newborn baby. That pup could have bitten her and she would not have retaliated. It was a baby, she knew it was a baby, and she treated it as a baby.

We had another dog, named Buck. He was a medium-sized, mature animal and not particularly friendly with strangers. Buck and Nguli formed an amazing friendship. Buck became very devoted and protective of Nguli. If Nguli needed to be disciplined, as she did at times, Buck could get ugly about it. And Nguli loved Buck and would try to protect him. If we tried to correct either one of them we had to deal with them both. If I was correcting Buck, Nguli would try to hold my hands and intervene.

When Buck and Nguli would play together it was hilarious. Nguli would grab his tail and drag him by it, or grab one of his legs to bring him down. In the meantime he would playfully bite her ears, arms, legs, and any other parts presented. They would roll and tumble, bite and growl, scream and carry on, but they were true friends. Buck would stay by her cage for a good part of every day.

One evening a visitor dropped by to see us, rather late for a visit, but we thank God that he did. When our guest came through our gate he saw a huge infestation of driver ants in our yard. They were everywhere. It was the largest attack of driver ants that I have ever seen, and they were all over Nguli's cage.

When our visitor told me, I ran out of the house, down the stairs, and into the back yard through the ants, unlocked her cage, and carried her to the veranda of the house. There we quickly began to pull all the ants off her. Fortunately, I had reached her in time. She was unhurt. Of course, I had to get the ants off myself as well.

We arranged to keep Nguli on the veranda for the next two weeks, because it took two weeks to kill the ants. That night, my wife and I and several Sierra Leoneans began the epic battle. We fought with gallons of insecticide, gallons of kerosene, boiling water, and fires. We fought until well after midnight and hardly made a dent in them.

The next day, armed with an insecticide spray pump, I attacked them again. I would forge a path through them, killing them by the thousands, but they fought back, dropping out of the trees on me and closing the path I had cleared behind me, entirely encircling me. After a while I would have to fight my way back to the house, get the ants off me, and reload my spray pump.

Driver ants give the definite impression of being an intelligent, organized, and militant army. I have seen them do amazing things working as a group, as a team to accomplish a common goal. For instance, these ants climb trees and cut down leaves that become boats to ferry whole groups of ants across water barriers. It sounds unbelievable, but it really happens.

After two weeks of major war, I won. My back yard was literally black with the corpses, millions of them. The army was now dead or had moved on. Thank the Lord, they never got into our house. After two weeks on our veranda Nguli returned to her own home, her cage in the yard.

She continued to gain strength and agility. She learned to ride a skateboard and resented it when my son wanted his skateboard back. She could run with fair speed, and in a tree her arm and shoulder strength was impressive. She was totally unafraid of heights.

As her strength grew she became more than a match for her cage. It could not hold her anymore. She would take the heavy one-eighth-inch strands of wire mesh that formed the front and bottom of her cage and simply strip them apart. She would pull the strands loose from the mesh they were welded to—ping, ping, ping, ping. The boards, the posts, everything on her cage could be destroyed anytime she chose, and she chose daily to destroy it enough to get out and run free. Sometimes she would come to the house, open the door, and race in. Soon Abbie would be in hot pursuit, trying to catch her before she could get to our bed, which she loved to use as a trampoline. It was impossible to outrun her, but with planning and luck we could, after a lengthy, frustrating chase, corner her.

We did not mind her being loose, if she would stay in the yard. She would play fine, but when the time came to return her to her cage she would whine. If she could, she would run away. Catching her in the yard was a real circus. A group of us would scheme and plot how to trap her. There was a lot of running and sometimes some tree climbing to catch her.

A cement ledge protruded from the wall of our house and circled it at a height of fifteen feet. Sometimes Nguli would run out on that ledge and just sit there and look at us, thinking we would not go out on the ledge after her. But when Brother J. P. Hughes was staying at our house, he fooled her. He went out on the ledge after her.

When she knew she was cornered, she would give up quite submissively. This exercise took place too frequently.

Finally, Nguli's cage was nothing but a patchwork of repairs. It was hopeless, so I put her in a cement room attached to the garage. The room had a couple of windows that we kept open for her, and these windows had steel bars imbedded in the cement. Nguli pulled the bars out of the cement and removed the entire steel window and frame. It became obvious that she had become too strong to be kept in any cage that I could afford to build for her. I was feeling bad because she was locked up so much and because I was not giving her the time and attention that she craved. She was a good, lovable pet, but I was too busy.

Although I felt that I was abandoning her, one day I took Nguli to a man who exported chimpanzees for zoos and circuses and sold her to him. He commented that she was a particularly good-looking animal and suitable for a zoo or circus and would see that she was taken care of.

I turned and walked away from her after he put her in a cage, but I felt like a rat. Nguli loved me, and I was leaving her. I could hear her calling, but I just kept on walking. I did not look back. It was hard enough as it was.

We had Nguli for six years, and I will never forget the fun and affection that was Nguli. I could have released her to the jungle, but she knew nothing about how to survive there, and she would not have wanted to go anyway. We tried to do the best thing for her by providing her with a new home that would have the facilities and training appropriate for her needs.

NINETEEN

THE CONTINUAL REVIVAL in Sierra Leone kept us constantly involved with church building projects. The need for more church buildings was ever before us.

As new congregations came into being, whether in villages, towns, or cities, they needed a place to meet for worship. Some areas had a court barrie that could be used, sometimes a schoolroom would serve, and sometimes there was no shelter, so the people would meet in the open under a tree.

The members would carry a homemade bench or chair from their home to the designated meeting place where the seating, such as it was, would be shared with others. After the service the seats were carried back home.

Some of the congregations met like this for over ten years before they were able to get a church building. At the time of this writing over ten congregations were still without a roof over their heads.

In the villages of the interior it was relatively easy to acquire property for a church. Sometimes it would be donated and at other times there would be a small cost, but in either case the process was quick and painless.

Buying land in the capital was extremely difficult and dangerous. The government record of land ownership was in total chaos. Fraudulent "declarations of

ownership" and "conveyance" documents were everywhere. For every piece of land on the market, three to
five people claimed ownership. Some people made a
business out of selling land they did not own. Any
effort to search the title was frustrating and futile. Nevertheless, to try to safeguard ourselves we would check
with government land registers, survey offices, neighbors surrounding the land, and so on. In ninety percent
of land sale negotiations it would be discovered that
the seller did not own the property in question, or the
title was challenged by other parties. Local courts were
literally crammed with land ownership disputes. Consequently, when trying to buy land in Freetown, we
were always at risk of buying a court case instead of
land. A buyer could be halfway into a construction pro-
ject when somebody would show up to ask why he was
building on his land then tell him to get off his land
immediately.

God protected us over and over again from unscrupulous people trying to bilk us out of church monies. We
never lost a piece of land or a church building, but on a
number of occasions we stopped just short of commit-
ting ourselves to land purchases that would have meant
the loss of much money. At the eleventh hour, over and
over again, we received information that kept us from
being the victim of crooks.

Many church organizations entirely gave up trying to
acquire land in Freetown. They could not find any for
sale, or the land they wanted had several parties claiming
ownership, or they bought land and then lost the land
and their money in a subsequent court case. The frustration, risk, and hassle involved in dealing with real estate
caused many church leaders to state publicly that they
would not build a church in the capital city.

But God was with us, and we were blessed to acquire

a number of pieces of beautiful land. Some of it was truly prime land ideally located and reasonably priced.

In 1996, the United Pentecostal Church owned ten pieces of property in Freetown and seventeen pieces in the interior, but these were not nearly enough. We had, in various stages of construction, seventeen church buildings. We had over fifty congregations, which meant half of them did not have even the beginning of a place to worship.

Our people were so desperately poor that the cost of the nails alone would have bankrupted some of the congregations. Still, we pressed them to put every cent, every drop of sweat and blood and time into their church that was possible. It was necessary. Their investment tied them to the church. They would only value what they had paid dearly to obtain. We were willing to help them, but only after they had demonstrated their own willingness to make real sacrifices to have a church.

When we had fund-raising rallies, over and over again I watched as people who lived in rough mud shacks with dirt floors danced down the aisles to the offering plates to give their money. They commonly came numerous times to give again and again. They came singing and shouting to give to the work of God, counting each act of giving as an expression of worship to Jesus Christ. They gave away their transportation money to get home from the rally, the next day's food money, the pittance they had set aside to buy used clothes, and they did it with joy. They gave until they had nothing left to give.

I saw a poor, deformed woman crawl down the church aisle to the altar bench where the offering plates had been placed. She could not see to the top of the altar, so she lay on her back, stretched her hand up to the offering plate, and gave her gift to God. Then, with joy, she crawled back to her place in the congregation.

Yet, when the rally was over, the total funds raised were announced, and the crowd, happy over the many leones given, was dismissed in prayer, I would look with mixed feelings at the offering. They had truly given to their power and beyond their power. They had given sacrificially, beautifully, gloriously, and even inspirationally. That made me happy. I loved them for their beautiful giving. I was pleased that the grace of God worked in them to give, but I was sad to see the meager value of the total offering, because it could do so little towards meeting the needs. The total offering in terms of U.S. dollars would vary from ten to twenty dollars, enough to buy three boards.

They did not give above their regular monthly expenses or obligations. They never had money in excess of bare necessities, and it was that money they gave. And when I refer to bare necessities they must be defined differently than in First World countries. They do not include a washing machine or dryer, electricity, piped-in water, carpets, draperies, a stove, heating or cooling, a car, a telephone, or a recliner. They don't even include a floor, a ceiling, shoes, school for their children, or medical help for the dying. They do not include paint on the mud walls or fertilizer for a lawn. There are no gifts for birthdays, anniversaries, or Christmas. Children do not have toys, and pets are a luxury unaffordable and unjustifiable. They cannot put money on pets when their children lack most things that we Americans consider necessities. Their diet is restricted to rice every day of their life, except when they cannot afford rice; then they eat inferior alternatives, or they do not eat at all.

Such were the people who gave at our rallies. The total leones may have only equaled ten to twenty dollars, but their sacrifice was equal to tens of thousands of dollars.

Still, the sellers of building materials did not look at

the value of this sacrifice. Instead, they looked at a required number of leones to meet the fixed price for the materials needed to build. Consequently, we appealed to our American churches to help our Sierra Leonean brethren to do what they could not do for themselves.

The churches that we built in the villages were simple mud-block structures with a light plaster of cement to cover the mud and protect it from the rain. The buildings had no ceiling, no glass windows, no covering over a bare cement floor, no finely finished woodwork, no bathrooms, no drapes, no Sunday school rooms, no electricity, no nice pews, and so on. Yet the people were thrilled over their new church. The entire village celebrated.

American construction workers would have had quite an adjustment to make in Sierra Leone. There we did not have ready-mix cement, power tools, ready-made scaffolding, kiln-dried lumber, or craftsmen trained in American methods of construction. Consequently, walls commonly were not plumb, nor were rooms square, nor were things level that were supposed to be level. Close was considered good enough, and sometimes even not close was considered good enough. Boards were cut randomly and crookedly. The people did not seem to understand why we Americans are so particular, why we want everything just right.

Yet I must give credit where it is due. I have seen tradesmen work extremely hard, without the benefit of any labor-saving devices or machinery, in the sweltering heat and humidity of the equatorial climate.

When we built in the city, by law, we had to use better materials. We could not put up permanent structures with mud walls. Cement was used throughout. We used wood to support the roof and for doors, but we avoided wood wherever possible because of the prevalence of dry rot and termites. Of course, better materials meant higher costs, but there was no alternative if we were to have churches in the city.

One day, when we were discussing the problems related to obtaining church buildings, it dawned on me that while we and other Christian organizations were struggling to acquire land and construct church buildings, Muslim mosques were everywhere in Sierra Leone, in every village and in every community in the towns and cities. I asked our pastors, "How is it that every village has a mosque, but the people cannot build a church? How is it that there is money to erect structures for Islam, but there is none for churches?"

The answer I received was enlightening: "No, Brother O'Keefe, the difference does not lie with the people of Sierra Leone. These mosques are here because Muslims of developed countries give the money for their construction."

This simple revelation was stunning. It should have been obvious, but the obvious often goes unnoticed or unconsidered. Muslims of the world were pouring millions, even billions, of dollars into the propagation and establishment of their religion. Consequently, every village and community in Sierra Leone had a mosque.

So I prayed, "Lord, help us. Your church has always grown in the face of opposition and in spite of obstacles. You own the wealth of the world, far more than all the oil-rich Arab countries of the earth combined. You are Jehovah-Jireh, the Lord who supplies. Help us to build churches for the name of Jesus."

TWENTY

WHILE WE WERE on our second furlough we received some disquieting news that our leading national preacher in Sierra Leone, the man who had come with us from Liberia, faced charges of conduct unbecoming to a minister. Of course, we were greatly concerned. We leaned much on this man for assistance in the mission, and we sincerely loved him as a son. It would be heartbreaking to have him fall.

After several more weeks I received another letter telling me that the charges had been investigated and dismissed. The acting superintendent in charge of the investigation assured me that he had personally checked into the matter and that the charges were groundless. The man was innocent.

It was a relief to hear that he had been acquitted, exonerated by a thorough investigation. People who had prayed over the matter declared that God had impressed them by His Spirit that he was truly innocent.

He had been declared innocent by the National Board of the United Pentecostal Church of Sierra Leone; therefore, I accepted that verdict. If he had been declared innocent, then he was to be treated as innocent.

I loved this man. He had been my right hand. We had worked together for years. He had opened many doors, had tutored my son, had lived in my home. He lived among my sons, and we had treated him like a son.

I was glad when he was declared innocent, because I wanted to believe he was innocent. I wanted to believe it because it would have a devastating effect on the work if it were otherwise.

As time would reveal, however, he was not innocent. He was very guilty, guilty of far more than anyone could have guessed.

We completed our furlough and began our preparations to return to Sierra Leone for our third term of service. There was much to do in buying, packing, storing, labeling, delivering, and shipping a container of goods to supply our needs for the next four years. I went through the required final orientation at headquarters. We tended to the numerous loose ends that come into everybody's life but tend to bunch up in a missionary's life and present themselves as a group during furlough time.

Once again we had to leave a son. Our youngest, Don, would be remaining in America. Sometimes, I felt almost sick with concern for his welfare. He had his two older brothers to help him, but he seemed too young, too inexperienced. Yet he was determined to be a man and to make his way in the adult world. What were we to do? We prayed, we wept, we hurt, and we committed him into the hands of God.

At the airport in San Francisco we said our good-byes to all our children, their wives, and our grandchildren. Tears were shed, encouraging and endearing words spoken, letters promised, and embraces made. With mixed emotions we boarded the plane in San Francisco for our third term in Sierra Leone.

We were met at Lungi International Airport by the Ramsey family and a good group of our national pastors. It was a happy reunion. There existed the kind of bond that is created between soldiers who have been on the frontlines of battle together, who have shared foxholes, who have seen the whites of the enemy's eyes, who have seen the blood and gore, and who have seen their comrades die around them. We had survived together. We had won many battles together. We had shared experiences, struggles, and victories. We were bound by a multitude of shared memories, which really meant we had shared life devoted to a common cause, the evangelization of the country, the exaltation of the name of Jesus Christ.

We quickly settled back into the work, pleased with the overall progress in our absence. We had returned in November, but the World Conference was to take place in February, just a few months away. Sierra Leone had qualified as one of the foreign fields eligible for representation at this conference, and money had been saved to send a national delegate. We were anticipating the trip.

The national treasurer was selected as the national delegate to represent Sierra Leone. He would be traveling to the World Conference with us.

The conference was in Manila, in the Philippine Islands, and it was a great conference with hundreds receiving the Holy Ghost. The facilities, the food, the service, everything was excellent.

During the time we were in Manila I began to notice an attitude problem with our national treasurer. I assumed that something was troubling him, some personal problem.

When the conference was over we stopped en route to Africa in California. While there we spent a few days with my sons and bought some items for our return to Africa. During one of our shopping trips our national treasurer accidently left some paper in our car. My wife, not knowing what it was, picked it up and read it. We were shocked! We could not believe it! We did not want to believe it, but it was right there in front of our eyes. Love notes. And not written to his wife. There was also a list of things that he was buying for a woman. We knew from comments he had made that these purchases were not for his wife.

We confronted him with the paper when he returned. His reaction was a dead giveaway, but he tried to smooth over the obvious with explanations that were unbelievable.

When we returned to Sierra Leone and settled in again our guard came to me. He said that he wanted to tell me about some things that had happened during our recent furlough. He told a sordid story of sin, debauchery, nightly immorality, continuous adultery, and licentiousness. It was the story of the treasurer's conduct while we were on furlough.

It was enough. I started an immediate investigation. Because this minister had so much influence within the mission, I felt that it was important to have a very strong case if we were to take action against him.

I was in for further shocks. As the investigation progressed, a veritable landslide of evidence and witnesses came forth. The charges mounted up even though we entertained no charges not supported by two or more witnesses.

The National Board came together to consider the charges, and because this was a judicial matter with charges against a board member, we handled the matter with special care. This man was in a powerful, influential position, and he was a popular leader. Therefore, we invited other ministers who had nothing to do with the case to serve as impartial witnesses of the proceedings.

During the trial the treasurer was buried beneath the avalanche of evidence. Witness after witness supplied consistent proof of wrongdoing. The accused did not even bother to defend himself.

The board excused themselves to confer, to come to a verdict concerning guilt or innocence, and, if the verdict was guilty, to determine the punishment. The deliberations were brief because the case was clear. Unanimously he was declared guilty of six charges of adultery and fornication and one charge of sedition. In accordance with our rules the penalty was clear. He was to be put out of the fellowship.

The board reentered the place of the trial and called the group to order. The accused heard the verdict: "Guilty!" He heard the sentence: "Disfellowshipped." He displayed no sorrow, regret, or humility. Instead there was virulent anger and venomous malice.

It was clear from his spirit and demeanor that he intended to fight. He would not submit humbly to this disciplinary action. He intended to make trouble.

We immediately confiscated the mission motorcycle on which he had ridden to the trial. He relinquished the key only when we made it emphatically clear that he would not be allowed to leave with it.

Every good thing we had ever done for him, every display of love or kindness, every benefit that had ever been provided, everything was buried beneath his shame and bitter hostility, lost in the blindness brought on by sin. He intended trouble, and he did make trouble. He intended to attack us in every conceivable way. He intended revenge for his exposure and shame, but we did not realize the extent to which he would go.

TWENTY-ONE

W HEN THE LEADING national church official is disfellowshipped, the disruptive, divisive news is
bound to travel fast. Consequently, we called a meeting
for the very next day and invited all our ministers within
reasonable distance to attend.

At the appointed time a large group of ministers
attended. Unfortunately, the disfellowshipped minister
was also present, and with him was a group of angry
church members.

They were advised that they were not invited to this
meeting, but they then became abusive and refused to
leave. Consequently, we endeavored to go ahead with
our purposes. We explained that the purpose of the
meeting was not to decide a case but rather to announce
the outcome of a case. We then announced that the minister had been disfellowshipped.

The hostile group began to shout and disrupt the
meeting. They demanded an immediate retrial then and
there with themselves as the judges. They refused to recognize the chair and total chaos ensued with name calling, accusations of betrayal, and serious threats of
physical violence, insomuch that chairs were lifted and
brandished as weapons. It was without a doubt the
worst meeting I had ever attended in my life. I could not
believe the conduct of some of these church members.

Could people change this much this fast? The Holy
Ghost did not act like this. Again and again I tried to
regain order, but to no avail.

The hostile group was adamant. They were not going
to accept the authority of the National Board and they
were not going to accept the verdict or sentence given
concerning the minister. They had been thoroughly poisoned by him and refused to listen to reason. It was an
impasse.

Their refusal to acknowledge the recognized authority of the church had to be dealt with, or the organization
would be seriously undermined. They had to cooperate
with the disciplinary action resulting from the judicial
procedure, or we would lose control of ministerial discipline.

We felt that there was no viable alternative but to present an ultimatum to all present. They could choose to
follow the guilty minister and withdraw from the United
Pentecostal Church, or they could accept the church's
authority and continue in unity and cooperation. The
matter was brought to an open declaration by every minister present. Unfortunately, three ministers chose to
resign and follow the guilty minister.

The meeting was dismissed and Brother Ramsey,
many other pastors, and I got into our car to leave. The
car was repeatedly kicked as we drove off. They were not
going to let the matter end here.

The next day was Sunday. The guilty minister and the
three pastors who resigned seized five of our churches and
refused entrance to any loyal United Pentecostal person.
Next, they sent members of their group to each of our
churches in the interior to try to bring about a general
breakaway. In this they failed. Nobody else joined them.

About a week later I received a formal letter from the
national Ministry of Labor demanding my presence at a

meeting. When I reached the Ministry of Labor I was ushered into an office of one of the functionaries, where I asked why I had been summoned. It was explained to me that complaints had been filed by the disfellow-shipped minister and his followers. We were accused of having wrongfully dismissed them from employment.

I was then given an opportunity to present the truth of the situation. I explained that the men in question had never been employees of the United Pentecostal Church, that the chief filer of the complaint had been barred from the ministry after a fair trial, and that the other men had not been dismissed but had publicly resigned from the United Pentecostal Church.

At this point the man questioning me laid aside any pretense of courtesy and impartiality. He immediately began a vociferous attack, stating that my position was nothing but a subtle subterfuge to deny men the rightful benefits of employment. He went on to give a well-rehearsed, well-worded presentation of a political, social, and economic ideology straight out of Patrice Lumumba University in Russia, a thoroughly communistic dialectic.

I was told in no uncertain terms that I must reinstate the ministers and pay them benefits and damages. I realized that further discussion was futile. I politely explained that I felt the need to have a lawyer represent us in the matter.

I had never in my entire life asked a lawyer to represent me in anything, but I was a foreigner in a foreign country with foreign ways. I needed a qualified spokesman.

Next, the guilty minister went to a lawyer, a fine man, to ask him to mediate our differences. Out of courtesy to the lawyer, I went to explain the situation. I explained about the man's dismissal, our judicial procedure, and the grounds for his dismissal. The man had told the lawyer prior to my coming that he had been unfairly tried and given no chance to defend himself, that we had dismissed him for ulterior motives, and that I was guilty of mistreating the pastors and of embezzling the mission funds. I patiently explained the truth, how that only the minister and three others had left our church, and I offered to show the mission financial records to the lawyer. I explained that we would not give the minister a new trial just because he demanded one. He had been fairly tried and proven abundantly guilty. There were no grounds for a retrial.

In the lawyer's office the guilty minister said that he had misunderstood about the finances and admitted that he was wrong in his accusation.

I was first to leave the meeting. I went down the stairs and waited for the guilty minister to come. When he did, I told him I still loved him and encouraged him to repent and get back in church. He walked away without speaking to me and continued to spread the slanderous charge of embezzling. Later, to protect me against this charge our regional field supervisor, Brother E. L. Freeman, signed a legal affidavit declaring that my handling of the finances was in agreement with organizational policy.

Unfortunately, this lawyer did not want to be involved with our case. He declined to represent either party.

I did engage another attorney to respond to the Ministry of Labor for us, which he did most effectively. He simply called the gentleman and told him that this was a civil matter that would be settled in court and that consequently we would not meet with him again. That was the end of our problem with that government office.

Next, I received a serious threatening letter from a lawyer hired by the ex-minister and his followers stating that I would be jailed if I did not report to his office and settle all his client's claims for damages to his satisfaction. I was given seventy-two hours to comply or face the consequences.

Again, I went to the attorney who had helped me with the Ministry of Labor. I showed him the letter I had received and asked for his advice. He expressed shock at the letter and said that it was unethical for such a letter to have been written and that I could not and would not be jailed. He telephoned the other attorney and upbraided him for his tactics, and it was settled then and there that all future correspondence should go to our attorney.

The ex-minister and his followers sent people to our home pretending sympathy for our situation, who then offered us "friendly advice" to leave Sierra Leone quickly, because our enemies had plans to attack us, and that much harm could come to us unless we escaped. When these people came, we did not always know if they were sincere or just trying to scare us off. Nevertheless, we could not simply leave. We could not abandon the church to the attacks of a group of renegades. We settled ourselves to face things, come what may.

We were deeply concerned about the churches that had been seized and felt uncertain as to what we could do. I wanted to handle things in a Christian way. Should we just bear the loss and forget it? I met with the National Board and told them of the decision we had to make, and their response was unequivocal. The property, the churches, the furniture, and everything that had been seized belonged to the United Pentecostal Church. Much money, time, and effort had been invested in those churches, and inasmuch as I was the national superintendent it was my responsibility and duty to safeguard the organization's property. Thus we pressed on with the steps necessary to recover our churches.

TWENTY-TWO

THE DISFELLOWSHIPPED minister permanently separated from his wife and sent her back to her people. Realizing that we faced a serious legal challenge, we began to gather all the evidence possible to substantiate our actions. We therefore sent two of our pastors to ask her to sign a sworn affidavit concerning her husband's adultery. She readily agreed, and we gave her the money to cover her travel expenses. When she reached Freetown she willingly signed the statement and then went to stay with friends in the Freetown area.

Somehow, the ex-minister found out what she did, how I do not know. He could not find his wife but knew she was in the city. He desperately wanted to locate her in order to intimidate her, to prevent her from hurting him. He went to the Criminal Investigation Division, the C.I.D., and accused our national secretary and me of kidnapping his wife.

I was shocked when the C.I.D. man came to my house to arrest me and the national secretary. The agent began to question me about the supposed kidnapping. I told him that there had been no kidnapping, that the woman had traveled of her own free will, had in fact traveled alone to Freetown, and was presently of her own free will staying in Freetown.

He then asked if we had given her money to travel to

the city, and I said we had. He then told me it was against the law to give another man's wife money to travel. At this point it was clear that the agent was making up laws as he went along. I suspected that he had been bribed or was a personal friend of the ex-minister. He intended then and there to take us to C.I.D. headquarters.

He had no vehicle, so we got in my Sheaves for Christ Mitsubishi, and headed toward town, but instead of going to C.I.D. I drove straight to our lawyer's office. Somehow I got that agent to go up with me to see the lawyer. When our lawyer heard the frivolous charges he picked up the telephone, called the national director of the C.I.D., and told him what his agent was doing. That was one very frightened agent. He was told to report immediately to the director. He left the office with his tail between his legs and never troubled us again. Yet, strangely enough, the wife still had to report to C.I.D. to make a formal statement that she had not been kidnapped.

The ex-minister next brought charges against our national secretary in tribal court. Fortunately, in the capital city, tribal court only has authority over a person if he recognizes its authority by answering the summons. We did not answer the summons, and the tribal court was powerless to pursue the matter further.

Then I received a letter from the Ministry of Social Welfare requiring my presence at a meeting regarding our church matters. I went, but I went well prepared. I went with the entire National Board, other preachers, and our attorney. When we arrived for the meeting we were courteously received. Word had reached the ministry that our church was operating as an unincorporated body, without a ruling board, without constitution and bylaws, and that we had arbitrarily dismissed fifteen preachers. This information was presented to us by open-minded, fair people in a polite manner. I responded that we were legally incorporated and offered to present our constitution and bylaws. I then asked the National Board to stand and explained that this was our ruling board. We explained that we had not dismissed fifteen preachers, but only one, and for just cause. Our attorney then explained the background of the malicious charges.

At this point the head of the meeting was angry with our accusers and ordered them out of the office. We received apologies for having been troubled and were allowed to go.

Because we were expecting further attacks, we continued with our efforts to protect ourselves by accumulating additional evidence that justified our dismissal of the renegade minister and our refusal to reinstate him or his followers. When we heard that they had joined another mission group, we checked into the story. It was true. The disfellowshipped minister was appointed as the superintendent of the Sierra Leone branch of the organization, and the three preachers who had resigned were all given national positions. The church had its headquarters in Liberia and was led by a well-known local figure whose character was publicly held in question. The group had been receiving considerable financial support from an American church that was internationally famous, but which was cutting off support because of issues of immoral conduct.

The disfellowshipped minister had told his followers that the new group's doctrinal position was the same as the United Pentecostal Church. Although they had left our organization, they still wanted our message.

I did not believe that the doctrine was the same. Brother Ramsey and I took a trip to Liberia, where we joined the missionary there, Brother Stewart. We then made an appointment to talk with the leader of the other mission. We were courteously received, and after greetings and casual pleasantries we told him why we had come. He acknowledged that our ex-minister had joined them. We then began to question him. Was he aware that the man had been disfellowshipped for adultery and sedition? No! He had given an entirely different account of events. Was he aware that the man was telling Sierra Leoneans that his new mission was going to build a hospital, a college, primary and secondary schools, and churches, buy vans and buses, and give each preacher a big salary? No! He had never told him any such thing. Was he aware that the property presently in the hands of the ex-minister actually belonged to the United Pentecostal Church and that we were taking steps to recover it? No! He thought that these properties would come to his mission with the men.

We then told him that the ex-minister was telling his people that our two groups were doctrinally the same, so we asked if we could politely question him to ascertain his doctrinal position. He was agreeable. As we questioned him point by point, he made it clear that he was a trinitarian; he did not accept the Oneness view. He did not baptize in Jesus' name. He did not believe that tongues was the evidence of receiving the Holy Ghost. He did not accept our holiness standards. He seemed quite concerned about the discrepancies between the ex-minister's statements and ours and assured us that he would check into the matter.

We then returned to Sierra Leone to tell our people what we had discovered. After some months, the breakaway element parted company with the Liberian-led group. Of course, none of the advertised promises were realized. Shortly afterwards, they affiliated with yet another mission and again declared that the doctrine was the same as ours. It was not.

The rebels then went boldly to our Bible college and tried to persuade students to leave our church. When they were not favorably received, they tried to pick fights with both students and staff. They stood in the open area in front of the college shouting, insulting, and challenging any or all of the students to fight them. Finally, they left, gloating over their manliness because no one had answered their challenge.

On separate occasions representatives of two of the congregations that had been seized came boldly into our compound with letters declaring their withdrawal from the United Pentecostal Church because we had "abused" their pastors. These letters were supposedly signed by all the members of the congregations. That was not true. Many of the signatories did not know how to write; others when questioned later said they had never even heard of the letter and that they had signed nothing. The letters were covered with forged signatures. After rudely delivering these letters and amid loud shouts, slanders, and insults the rebels left the neighborhood.

These two letters later proved to be a real help in our endeavors to recover our church property. The rebels later tried to deny the letters and their content, but we kept them safely in our possession.

TWENTY-THREE

I T HAD BECOME clear that the disfellowshipped minister would go to any limit to get revenge on us for his humiliation. I felt that his actions displayed such a degree of unconscionable behavior, such unscrupulous conduct, that he had crossed a line in his dishonest attacks against the church, its ministers, and leaders, a line of no return. I could see no place of repentance for him. I felt bad that it was so. I did not want it to be so, but I felt it was.

Several weeks later a young man came to my home with a court summons. The ex-minister was with him. I was served with papers accusing me of criminal conduct. I was truly shocked. I was accused of having assaulted the man resulting in bodily injury. Of course, it never happened, but there were no limits to his conduct in attacking me.

It seemed unbelievable that these people with whom I had worshiped, who had once displayed the love of God, who had been my brothers and sisters in Christ, who had received a new-birth experience, could have so changed, could be so virulent, so dishonest, even cruel and vicious, so shockingly uncaring about scruples or principles. But they had been so thoroughly poisoned by twisted and warped presentations that reason was lost in a lust for vengeance.

The same lawyer who had written the threatening letter to me was to represent the ex-minister in this court case. I had never been in a court case in my life, not even as a spectator, and certainly never as a defendant. I was innocent of the charge. The incident supposedly had taken place at the meeting conducted to announce the man's dismissal. There were twenty preachers present at that occasion who were prepared to testify that it never happened. Missionary Jerry Ramsey was witness to my innocence. Our attorney assured me that the case would be ruled in my favor.

In the meantime it became evident that litigation was going to be essential on a different but related matter. Even though the breakaway faction had joined several missions since leaving us, they continued to claim that they were still members of the United Pentecostal Church. The leader claimed that the National Board did not have any authority to dismiss him, and his followers loudly declared that they had never resigned or withdrawn from fellowship. They claimed full continued membership and a full right to be in possession of our property. Therefore, it was essential to have a court declare our legal right to determine who was a member or minister in the United Pentecostal Church. The question was absolutely critical. It went to the very core of our ability to exist, to function as an organization in Sierra Leone. The question had to be settled in our favor, or we could maintain no control whatever over conduct, morals, doctrine, property ownership, or church membership. Consequently, a second court case began, which took place concurrently with the criminal charges against me.

In the meantime our enemies went to the permanent secretary of the President of Sierra Leone. They appealed to this man to have us summarily deported from the country. I was told about it, and knowing the political corruption that existed, I knew that I could not ignore this threat. Fortunately, the first vice president of Sierra Leone lived only two blocks from my house. My wife and I made an appointment to see him and in a few days were granted audience. He was friendly and cordial and listened patiently to our problem and the threat we were facing of deportation. We were not a little comforted when he assured us that he would not allow us to be deported and that if our enemies wanted to use political power to attack us he would show them who had political power. Praise the Lord!

Before court proceedings had begun, the ex-minister went to one of the local newspapers and gave them the story of our differences from his biased viewpoint. The story ended up on the front page: "Pastors in Court: Chaos in Church."

When we later went into court, our attorney showed the newspaper to the judge. He was incensed and ordered the paper's editor brought immediately to the courtroom. When the editor arrived, the judge threatened to jail him then and there. The man was frightened and apologetic, so the court was merciful and allowed him to depart after a strict warning never again to print such biased articles, especially when the facts of the case were still in the process of being ascertained by the court.

It was a moral victory, but the article had been printed and published. The damage had been done.

The case wherein I was charged with criminal assault was greatly prolonged due to several changes in judges. Each time a judge was transferred or changed (four times), the case had to be started over again from the beginning. Even when the case proceeded with a single judge the postponements and adjournments were many.

Our attorney suggested that we only use three or four witnesses to substantiate our case rather than weary the court with the twenty witnesses available to us. We deferred to his expertise and notified our witnesses to be ready to testify.

Of course, the prosecution presented its case first. The ex-minister was the first witness. He placed his hand on the Bible and repeated the oath, then proceeded with a string of malicious lies told so convincingly that he must have sold his soul to put on such a performance. He told the court that I had approached him in the Guy Street meeting and with anger violently pushed him so that he fell over several benches and on to the floor, and that he suffered cuts and bruises as a result. His supporting witness confirmed his account of the events.

The defense was then given its opportunity to present its case. I went to the witness stand and related the truth that the whole case was a malicious fabrication from the beginning to end, that there had been no assault, and that there had been no injuries. Three more ministers substantiated my testimony.

There was no evidence of bodily injury, no medical statements of any kind. Evidence was presented that the ex-minister and his group had not been invited to the meeting but forced their way in, refused to leave, and refused to behave after their arrival. Evidence was presented to show motive for malicious prosecution. Evidence was presented to prove that their conduct had been violent, not ours.

We left the court to wait for weeks while the judge determined my guilt or innocence. In the meantime our attorney assured me of victory. He was completely confident. He said that the weight of the evidence and precedent was on our side.

While we waited for the outcome of the case, matters

continued on the civil case concerning the breakaway ministers' status with the United Pentecostal Church. This case was considerably more complicated because our organizational constitution and bylaws had to be examined, and corporate law was involved.

The judge in the case was a perceptive, intelligent man who repeatedly caught the opposition telling lies. Openly in the courtroom he called the opposing attorney a liar. He also caught the ex-minister lying. For instance, the man, after declaring he was still a member of our organization, had his name announced over the radio as a minister and speaker for a different mission. The judge was listening to the radio when the announcement was made. That announcement was entered as evidence. The statement of resignation from the organization that we had kept in our possession was presented as evidence, as were the minutes from the trial.

After all the evidence was presented, we had to wait several more weeks for the verdict.

TWENTY-FOUR

SERIOUS DIVISION began to develop among the break-away group due to things coming to light. The leader had steadfastly declared himself innocent of all charges of adultery, but it became known that the separation from his wife was final. Next, he proposed marriage to one of the women with whom he had been conducting an adulterous relationship.

The ex-minister married again but never bothered to get a divorce from his previous wife. A few months later, he had his new marriage solemnized, this time in a Muslim ceremony. He had lost all perception of right and wrong.

His followers turned on him and literally drove him from the church. He would not be their pastor again. Yet they still remained united in their fight against the United Pentecostal Church.

Again, the opposition went to the newspapers and presented a deceitful account concerning church ownership and how we were trying to force innocent, rightful owners from their place of worship. The newspapers were unscrupulous. They made no effort to confirm the factuality of what they printed. They considered only one factor when printing a story: whether it would sell papers.

One of the pastors who resigned to follow the guilty minister drove his wife away, without grounds. There was no divorce, but he still took a new wife.

Finally, the day arrived to hear the verdict on the criminal charges against me. I went to the courthouse confident of the outcome and walked into the courtroom to await the calling of our case. In just a short time our case was called, and I stepped forward.

Under the British system of law, which is copied in Sierra Leone, there is a small wooden enclosure like a pen where those accused of crimes are made to stand throughout the trial. Thus far, I had not been required to go into this enclosure out of respect for my being a missionary, but then things changed. The new judge insisted that I be placed in the criminal's corral. An officer of the court opened the gate and I was ordered to step inside. When I stepped inside the enclosure, I realized that I was being treated as a criminal. I got a glimpse of what it must feel like to be led into a courtroom wearing handcuffs. I was wearing a suit, but I felt the same humiliation as if I had been wearing prison garments.

Some in the courtroom began to laugh and to mock me through the instigation of our opposition. The prosecuting attorney shouted to the galleries that I was a thief and had robbed the people of Sierra Leone of the financial help that Americans had sent for them. The statement was untrue and had nothing to do with the case. It was designed solely to incite the crowd against me. The courtroom was a circus.

I could do nothing but stand there and bear the insults, lies, and mockery being hurled at me. Humiliation lay upon me like a heavy weight. I was not guilty. The charges were complete fabrications made out of malice. The prosecution's witnesses had completely and deliberately perjured themselves. Reliable and respectable defense witnesses were seemingly ignored. I was being judged guilty of a crime that I had not committed.

It was not fair. Something in me raged that I had a right to justice, but I knew that there was not going to be any justice. There was not going to be any justice because a man who claimed to be a minister of the gospel dared to put his hand on the Bible, swear an oath that he would "tell the truth, the whole truth, and nothing but the truth, so help me God," and then spin a tale of lies in his effort to destroy me.

The attorney defending me had given me complete assurance that I would never be found guilty of the charges. He swore this on his reputation as a doctor of law. I would be vindicated.

As I stood in the dock the judge read the verdict: "Guilty as charged." I was stunned. I could not grasp it. I had been assured of a verdict of innocence. Again, the crowd at the circus rooted and hooted. Their tactics had won them a victory, and they gloried in my shame.

I wondered, Will I be sentenced to time in a Sierra Leonean prison? Sierra Leonean prisons are renowned for the horrible conditions inmates are made to endure. The death rate is atrocious. Men are crowded into rooms so tightly that they cannot lie down or even sit down. There are no bathroom facilities, and they often go days without food or water. The filth and stench are unimaginable.

And I thought about my wife: How will she cope with this? We must not hate. We must not be bitter. We must not generalize and blame a nation for the evil of a few. It hurt me to think of the hurt that my wife would experience. I wanted to protect her, but I seemed helpless to do so.

I thought of the bench full of newspaper reporters as they gleefully prepared their front-page stories with headlines reading, "Missionary Found Guilty of Assaulting Pastor." I wondered if the publicity would hurt the church and destroy my future ability to work there. I thought of the years of labor endeavoring to establish the church and wondered if it was all going to be in vain. It was the devil's hour. It seemed that I was down and demons were taking turns kicking me.

Yes, I thought of the years of sacrifice, living away from my children and grandchildren. I thought of the discomforts we had borne living in the tropics, doing without electricity and basic goods, of living in a primitive culture, of the intense poverty, the disease, the deprivations, the loneliness. And yes, I thought, Is this the thanks I get for having given my life and my family's lives to help these people? Is this the way they repay me?

As I stood in the dock the thoughts raced through my mind. In milliseconds thoughts were formed, erased, new thoughts formed, erased, new thoughts formed, erased.

I sought comfort by scanning my memory for passages of Scripture or Bible stories that would enable me to place my situation in the scope of history. I thought of Joseph, some of the prophets, and Paul, and I thought of Jesus Christ. Then I felt ashamed. Only this time my shame was not because I stood as a criminal in the dock being jeered by a hostile crowd, but because it dawned on me that compared to those in the Bible, compared to my Lord, I had suffered nothing. My moments of inconvenience and discomfort were not worthy to be compared to the agony of prophets, patriarchs, apostles, and especially not to that of my Lord Jesus Christ. Yet I had felt such grief, such humiliation, such moral outrage when I should have felt a holy sense of honor and privilege, when I should have held my head up high and rejoiced because I had been counted worthy to bear some small thing for His name's sake. Then, in my mind and in my heart, I said to Jesus, "I am sorry, Lord. You have a purpose in all of this. Teach me to trust You. Help me to walk through this trial with You and to glorify Your name."

Order was restored to the court. The judge was speaking again. The sentence was being read. The hostile and the curious hung on his words in the expectant silence. It was a charged atmosphere broken only by the words of the magistrate. The case was briefly summarized and then it came: "Suspended sentence!" A token fine was levied, which I never had to pay. I walked out of the court a free man.

Even though I had suffered no penalty, I had been found guilty. Our enemies continued their mocking and jeering as we left the courtroom. I wondered, What next, Lord? What will be in the newspapers? What new attacks will follow this? What course are we to take?

God did not see fit to explain the future to me, but He did encourage me to trust Him and to believe that somehow He was in control, that He was with me, and that I should just walk on believing Him.

TWENTY-FIVE

DURING THESE EVENTS I turned continually to God for strength and help. Every morning I was on my knees no later than 5:30 A.M. seeking the face of God. I was walking by faith, never knowing what new crises we would face or how to face them. I prayed for strength and love and patience, but I felt weak and vulnerable and hurt and anxious. I prayed, "God, help me to take one step at a time, to live one day at a time. God, give me strength for that one step, that one day."

As I prayed, seeking the face of God, with spiritual ears straining to hear His voice, desperately wanting and needing guidance and reassurance, I told the Lord what we were facing. I mixed my prayers with my tears and begged God to intervene lest the church be destroyed.

I tried to sort out my feelings. I wanted in all of this to be what He would have me to be. I felt that I should be more serene, more reconciled to eventualities, more trusting—I did not know what I should be. I just knew that I could not stand by idly while satanically inspired renegades destroyed the work of God.

We were being attacked from so many sides so continuously that we constantly expected new attacks. The tension was there day and night. Our night guards at our home stayed alert expecting physical attacks.

I did not know the answers, I did not know what

crises the future held, but I knew that Jesus did and that He held the answers. I was anxious, often even afraid. I had to face my fear and deny its demands. I had to stand and defend the church.

In this time of prayer, I conducted much self-examination, soul searching, and self-analysis. What are my motives? I asked myself. Are they pure? Are they vain and selfish? What are my real concerns? Is my concern sincerely a defense of the truth, of the church, and of Jesus Christ, or is it something more personal? Is it an egotistical battle to preserve the work of my ministry, my name, and my reputation? At this point I had invested a dozen years into the development of the Sierra Leonean church. I did not want to see it destroyed. I did not want to be a failure.

But it was more than egotism. This was my gift to my God and Savior. This church represented my life, my dedication, and my love for Him. I felt that I could endure the spoiling of my name if the work could survive. I did not want to stand in judgment empty handed before Him whom I loved supremely. Yes, there was a personal concern, but it was inextricably interwoven with concern for His church, with concern for His name. His name and His church must not suffer shame or loss. I believed after self-analysis that I was sincere. I did care about the souls of this nation, about the truth, and about the inestimable glory of Jesus Christ.

Every word of prayer, every moment of meditation was saturated with tears, with agonized pleas for God to help us, and with a childlike longing to hide in the cleft of the rock, the Rock of Ages.

One day, as I knelt at the couch in the parlor, the room began to lighten with the dawn. Immediately behind me on a coffee table lay a large display Bible. I turned to look at it. It was lying open, and as my eyes fell on its pages I began to read the first passage my eyes met. It said: "Fear thou not; for I am with thee: be not dismayed; for I am thy God: I will strengthen thee; yea, I will help thee; yea, I will uphold thee with the right hand of my righteousness. Behold, all they that were incensed against thee shall be ashamed and confounded: they shall be as nothing; and they that strive with thee shall perish. Thou shalt seek them, and shalt not find them, even them that contended with thee: they that war against thee shall be as nothing, and as a thing of nought. For I the LORD thy God will hold thy right hand, saying unto thee, Fear not; I will help thee" (Isaiah 41:10-13).

I felt His holy presence in the room and knew that my prayer had been heard. He had spoken to me from the pages of His Word. A promise that God had given to Israel was personalized and given to me. In the growing light of a new day I lifted my hands to the One who hears and answers prayer, and with streaming tears said, "Thank You, Lord Jesus! I love You, my God!"

A few days later, one of our pastors was attacked and had his head cut open with a carpenter's rip saw. These attacks were entirely unprovoked. Later that same pastor was hit on the head with a bottle and knocked unconscious.

TWENTY-SIX

A T LONG LAST, the day arrived for the verdict on the critical issue of church membership. I was deeply concerned. All logic said that we had an airtight case, but there was widespread corruption in the judiciary, so there was always cause for concern.

When the verdict was read, I figuratively held my breath. It seemed that my pulse and heartbeat went into suspension. I had learned not to be confident in court. Yet we had to win this one. We had to!

Point by point the judge read the verdict. The rebel minister and his followers were declared not to be members of the United Pentecostal Church. All church property was to be returned to us. Our church constitution and bylaws were upheld. They were to pay court costs.

We had won every single point. What a relief! What a weight off my shoulders! Thank You, Jesus!

Outside the courtroom I was confronted by the opposition. I did not want to talk with them. I just wanted to go home and tell my wife the good news, but they began to shout and insult me and the other faithful ministers. I felt that I would be assaulted right there in the courthouse, but our attorney came on the scene and ordered them to move on, and they did.

Sunday was two days later. We sent three of our preachers to attend each of the five churches that had been seized. They were met at the door in every case and refused entrance. Six of our pastors were violently assaulted, and all of them were sent away.

We had no choice but to report the matter back to the judge. An injunction was approved that barred any of the offending ministers or their agents from entering the property of the United Pentecostal Church.

The next Sunday the performance was repeated. Again, our ministers were refused entrance. Again, they were physically assaulted. The injunction was ignored, the judge and his court defied.

Again we reported the problem. This time the defiant preachers were held in contempt of court. Two of them were sent to jail, while a third was in hiding. Somehow the leader escaped being jailed.

The judge told us to go back and put new locks on the church doors, and to protect us while doing so he assigned five policemen and two bailiffs. We went back with new locks in hand. The opposition spotted our entourage and quickly ran through the neighborhood to alert their followers, who came running to the church. As we worked at replacing the locks, a hostile crowd gathered, a crowd poisoned with hatred. It became loud and unruly.

In just a little while the people became violent. The police could not control them. They began throwing dirt and stones. Our pastors had their clothes torn. They were cursed, spit on, kicked, stoned, slapped, and beaten. One of the rebel leader's close followers walked up and punched me in the face. The police grabbed him and put him in my car. At this point things were completely out of control. The police insisted that we leave immediately, which we did while stones followed us. Later two more of the rioters were arrested and jailed.

I wondered, God, is this never going to end?

The outcome of the riot was that the police brought charges against the arrested rioters. Another court case. Everything was poorly handled by the police. Records and statements were disorganized and presented incorrectly. The judge in the case was openly and obviously biased. The motion for a new judge was denied. One of the policemen called to be a witness denied that he had even been at the scene. All our witnesses, all preachers, were belittled and berated. The end result was that the man who had attacked me was fined about one U.S. dollar. The other defendants were declared innocent and set free. They left the courtroom laughing, joking, and mocking.

Then, on the instructions of the court, we tried to change the locks on one of the other seized churches. Again, there was a major riot. Again, the police could not cope with it.

Before we left we did get the locks changed, but to no avail. The locks were broken that same night and the church was entered. The culprits were seen breaking and entering. And the rebel leader was witnessed breaking the court injunction.

All of this was reported to the judge, who was more than a little upset at the repeated defiance of his authority.

Again there was another contempt case! This time the rebel leader did not escape. He was placed under bond to keep the peace for a period of six months. This is a common procedure under the British system of law and carries serious consequences for those who ignore its intent. The ex-minister was shaken. He knew he was in danger of going to prison if he continued his ways. In addition, the judge dictated that armed personnel should go to the defiant churches, close them, and guard them day and night. Only United Pentecostal people were to enter the property.

Finally, all the churches were back in our possession, but things were far from settled. We had possession, but we were prevented from using them.

One of the churches was designated as the venue for a fellowship meeting, and our people came from far and wide to attend, but the agents of the opposition also gathered a group. They made it clear that they intended to rush into the church the moment the doors were opened. Police were present but advised against opening the doors. Our people sang, prayed, and praised God by the roadside and then returned to their separate communities and homes.

It was a standoff. We had possession but could not use the buildings. And in order to maintain possession we had to keep the opposition out. The only alternative was to close and lock the churches in question. The government posted armed guards to protect us and our property. Those guards had to stay on duty day and night for two years.

On one occasion, we went into one of the churches to clean it. After cleaning it, we decided to take the church's musical instruments to our Bible college. We got them loaded in the car and I drove off. Others who had helped walked away, but one of our presbyters, Brother Kaitell, was the last to leave. He mounted his motorcycle and was driving away when a group of the opposition came around the corner of the church. He did not see them and was driving slowly. The group ran up behind him and knocked him completely off the motorcycle. One of them began to strangle him and beat him, while the others stole the motorcycle. The armed guard from the church tried to intervene, but they grabbed him and took his rifle from him. This intimidated him and it also shamed him. Finally, they quit beating Brother Kaitell and let him go, but without the motorcycle.

We reported the matter to the police, who recovered the motorcycle for us, but when they tried to arrest the person who had abused Brother Kaitell, he fled the country.

During the course of these events, I had been physically assaulted on five different occasions, and my car had been damaged. Our pastors had suffered many assaults. Yet I have to praise our people. They did not fight back. They turned the other cheek time and again. They suffered as Christians and gave a good testimony of the grace of God working in them. Brothers A. E. Chambers, James Sesay, Steven Mallay, John Samai, David Sesay, J. H. Kaitell, George Peters, Alfred Menefee, Egerton Jones, Samuel Kolie, and others suffered for the truth. They did not let the sight of their own blood deter them from standing for the truth.

TWENTY-SEVEN

I WAS QUITE SURPRISED when a delegation of nearly fifteen Muslims came to my home and asked to speak to me. I invited them in, and they explained their purpose in coming. They had seen the ongoing abuse we were suffering and they did not like it. They subtly let me know that the Muslim community was rather large and that it was ready to act on our behalf if I gave them the word. They were offering to make a physical attack on our enemies, and it was a very serious offer. People would be injured, and some could be killed. Of course, I could not agree to do that, but I was encouraged by the sympathy and concern that they expressed. I thanked them for their concern and politely rejected their offer.

On another occasion, a former professional boxer serving as the national boxing instructor offered to go teach our opposition some manners. Again, I had to decline the offer.

About this time Sierra Leone passed laws making it illegal to have any foreign currency in one's possession. That meant it was a criminal offense to own U.S. dollars. The government even made it illegal to have a foreign bank account. Tourists visiting Sierra Leone were jailed if they did not exchange all of their foreign currency within three days after entering the country, and their foreign currency was confiscated. Needless to say, tourism died immediately. Peace Corp personnel had all of their money confiscated. The U.S. Embassy and other embassies made formal complaint over this policy.

The C.I.D. began making surprise raids on homes and businesses suspected of having foreign currency. The disfellowshipped minister went to the C.I.D. and told them we had foreign currency. The C.I.D. showed up at my home about fifteen strong with a search warrant. They went all through our home and found a five-pound note of British sterling. That was all.

The agents admitted that the raid was a product of our enemies. A couple of them were very kind. One, a woman, said her children attended one of our Sunday schools. Another agent said his brother was one of our pastors. They were apologetic and tried to get the other agents out of the house as soon as they could. Finally, they left. But our privacy had been invaded. We were Americans and were used to the fierce protection of privacy provided by the U.S. Constitution. We don't realize how much we take such things for granted until they are taken away.

Next, the rebel minister and his cohorts appealed the court case that excluded them from the United Pentecostal Church. The appeals court had three judges hearing each case. No new evidence was admissible; they only reviewed the evidence already presented. They called no witnesses. Shortly after the proceedings got under way, the lead judge stated that it was unconstitutional to bar a person from the worship of his choice and that the injunctions barring our enemies from entering our churches must be eliminated.

The opposition took this to mean that they could come and repossess one of the churches that was functioning again. We expected trouble, so we invited plain-clothes policemen to attend the service as observers. It was fortunate that we did, because when the rebel group arrived they took over. They refused to be orderly and generally disrupted the service.

When we reported this development at the next court session, and the plainclothes police testified, the lead judge realized his error and qualified his stand. The other group could come to the church, but they could not conduct themselves other than as visitors in the assembly and must cooperate with the designated authorities of the church and respect the rules of the assembly. They never came again.

Since I was the superintendent most of the attacks had been directed at me thus far, but Brother Ramsey had his turn at being a target. During my furlough the rebel leader had approached Brother Ramsey with a vial of a substance that looked like dirt and asked him to take it to America for analysis to check for gold content. Brother Ramsey declined because doing so could have constituted an act of smuggling under Sierra Leonean law, but he offered to ask a local friend, a doctor of chemistry, to analyze it for him. The sample was quite small for a proper assay, so an additional quantity was requested. When the minister failed to respond, the matter was dropped and forgotten.

Then two years later the man demanded his gold. Of course, there was no gold. There never had been. The man threatened to go to court unless the gold or a large sum of money was given to him. It was nothing more than an attempt to extort money by threats. Brother Ramsey refused to give in to these threats.

Criminal charges were filed in magistrate court. Again, an unscrupulous media picked up the story. The newspapers shouted: "Missionary Steals from Parishioners."

Brother Ramsey was completely innocent, but he had

to prove his innocence. Too freely, people were allowed to make unsubstantiated, frivolous, and malicious charges as a means to harass others.

Inasmuch as the rebel leader had asked for an assay to ascertain the nature of the substance given to Brother Ramsey, he had to prove it was gold, but could not. The case was dismissed for insufficient evidence.

Criminal charges were dropped, but it was still possible for a civil suit to be filed. The Ramsey family had a special reason to be concerned about this threat. They were due to go on furlough. They had their airline tickets. Their flights were booked and seat assignments made. If the civil suit got filed before they departed, their passports would be seized to prevent them from traveling. Consequently, their travel plans were kept as quiet as possible. The criminal charges were dismissed against Brother Ramsey that morning, and the Ramsey family was on a British Airways flight that afternoon.

With the Ramsey family gone, my wife and I were the only United Pentecostal missionaries in the country. Of course, we missed them.

TWENTY-EIGHT

THROUGH THE BATTLES that had come our way and by our standing, staying, and facing them, a change began to take place in our United Pentecostal pastors, even on the National Board. They gave me a new and greater respect. More and more, Sierra Leoneans volunteered to step forward to fight the battles. The rebel leader had tried to put a racial tone into the court cases and make it seem like a white against black problem, but our black pastors made it clear: "This is black against black!" Of course, it was more than that; it was the church against the spiritual powers of hell.

Our common enemy had caused us to pull together, to have closer unity. The problems caused a mature leadership to develop.

The newspaper stories had caused the general community to be quite aware of the United Pentecostal Church in general and me in particular, and although the accounts had been negative, most people ignored the slanders and treated us like celebrities. The general public, for the most part, compared our conduct to that of our enemies and accusers and appreciated the integrity with which we had handled our affairs. The church and I received more respect than ever before.

We had been in nine different court cases, 110 court appearances, many meetings in government offices, many meetings in lawyers' offices, several major riots, many assaults, innumerable threats—all within five years. Normally each term of service did not exceed four years, but because of the critical litigation involving the work, we chose to extend our term for an additional year.

At long last we were seeing the light at the end of a dark tunnel. It had been a five-year war, a satanic campaign to drive us out of Sierra Leone and destroy the church, but King Jesus won this battle and His banner of salvation was waving gloriously over the battlefield. The enemy was in retreat and his forces in disarray.

Many good men and women had suffered. Blood had been shed, but it would serve as seed to raise up an army prepared to march against the very strongholds of hell.

We were wounded, dirty, and torn, but we were on the high ground now. A cool breeze had caused the clouds to drift away, and the sun was shining warm upon us. There we knelt and gave thanks to our Captain. He had not failed us. He had not left us alone on the battlefield. This was His church, His message, His name, and He had defended His own.

He had said that He would not leave us or forsake us. He said, "Go . . . and, lo, I am with you alway, even unto the end of the world." When we had felt alone, we had not been. He had never left us, not for one minute.

In the heat of the battle, in the thick of the fray, when darkness prevailed and confusion reigned, when all confidence in our own ability to survive the onslaughts was gone, a rider on a white horse, a rider called Faithful and True, whose name is called the Word of God, came and fought for us.

We were victorious, not proudly so, but humbly so. He had won, and we owed Him honor and praise. And that praise came forth not as a product of obligation but as the spontaneous response of a heart overflowing with love and gratitude, a heart trembling anew at the awesome reality of God.

The churches that had been closed and locked were reopened, and new congregations filled them. Our churches grew. Our Bible college began to receive widespread recognition as an excellent ministerial training center. One half of the military chaplains in the country were out of our college. The national police chaplain and his assistant were both graduates from our college.

Our insistence on integrity in the ministry had magnified respect for the message. All over the city people acknowledged us and treated us kindly. Lawyers, judges, and police treated us like celebrities. In a country where corruption and immorality in the ministry were the norm, our battle to purge such corruption had not gone unnoticed or unappreciated.

It was a great day when one of the groups that had rioted against us, a group that had perpetrated many of the most violent assaults, came to us and asked to be accepted back into the church. They acknowledged their wrong and promised to submit themselves to the conditions we would require.

We were not interested in revenge. These people had been poisoned and used by unscrupulous men. They had been lied to and misled. They had come to realize that and wanted to come back. We did not accept them as a group, but explained that any individual could return if he would come on a probationary basis and prove his sincerity. Although we had not accepted them as a group, most members of the group returned as individuals and eventually regained full membership.

One extremely violent young man who had been a leader in the riots asked to be accepted for training in the ministry. He was accepted. He was truly a changed man.

Our third term as missionaries had lasted five years,

and now it was furlough time again. There were still loose ends. Some problems were still unresolved, but the major battles had been fought and won; only the mopping up remained.

The appeal case was still pending, but the outcome seemed certain: our case was solid. The continuance of the case was no more than the spastic convulsions of a dying opposition.

As the airplane lifted off the runway, I looked through the window at the terrain below. I said an unspoken good-bye to the land that was part of me. It was a poignant moment made more so by the battles fought; by the literal blood, sweat, and tears; by the victories won in fierce spiritual combat. Below was the arena where the contest had been fought, where the foe had been vanquished. Standing with bloodied sword in hand, wounded, dirty, and worn, we figuratively heard the shouts of angelic spectators that occupied the stands in the coliseum of eternity. Yet, with a humbled and hungry heart, our eyes searched the stands for the approval of the King, for only in Him can we claim victory.

It seemed as if the arena itself had absorbed some of the holiness of God's Spirit, as if an aura of His presence remained, as if the battleground was made dear and holy by the manifestation of His power as the unseen, but ever-present, Gladiator.

As I looked down, my view contained more than the physical terrain. It also encompassed the holy arena where God had stood at my side to fight, where the common and profane had been made sacred by the blood of saints.

Good-bye, Sierra Leone, I thought. Good-bye, dear land touched by the kingdom of God. Good-bye, arena of sacred warfare.

TWENTY-NINE

WE ARRIVED BACK in San Francisco tired and excited. As the 747 taxied to the concourse, we spent the moments anticipating the reunion with our sons.

Mark and Tom were now married and had children of their own. We were anxious to use whatever time we could to be part of their life, to be a grandma and grandpa.

Finally, the plane stopped and the "Fasten Seatbelts" sign went off. Quickly, as if in a race, all were on their feet grabbing their carry-on luggage from the overhead bins. Coats were donned, and we quickly stepped into the aisles to establish our place in line to the exit.

At last the door opened and we inched down the aisle to the exit, saying good-bye to the stewardesses. Walking down the tube to the concourse, we strained to see the face of someone we knew, to see the first expressions of recognition. There they were! Fingers were pointing, arms waving, smiles glowing. The reunion was sweet.

The blur of activity demanded by deputational travel began: the visits, too brief, with family and friends; the business requirements; the travel from church to church; the conferences, and so on.

The travel was taxing, but there was a burning motivation to preach the great commission in every service, to preach the priority of missions. An intense anointing came upon me every time I preached that the cause of the Cross is an outreach for the unreached. We have a world to reach for Jesus Christ, and the hour demands urgency.

Invariably, family and friends plaintively asked if we were going to return to Africa again. Our sons and grandchildren did not want us to go back. Friends asked us to stay, but we could not. Some of them tore us apart with their appeal, but we could not.

The days passed and soon it was time to leave again. Good-bye, sons and daughters-in-law. Good-bye, grandchildren. Good-bye friends. Good-bye, America.

THIRTY

WHILE ON FURLOUGH, we received word that the rebels had given up their appeal case and ceased further attacks. It was the last gasp of the opposition.

We also received word that Sierra Leone had been invaded by an army of Liberian rebels. Sierra Leone was formally at war.

We arrived back in Africa on June 19, 1991, to begin our fourth term of service. One of our goals for this term was to build our national headquarters facility and a number of other city church buildings.

Construction started in earnest shortly after our arrival and occupied much of my time. Often we had several building projects going simultaneously. We were thrilled with erection of physical landmarks that would help establish the work and give it permanence until Jesus comes.

Construction was progressing well until the coup d'etat.

During the predawn hours of Wednesday, April 29, 1992, several truckloads of army troops from the battle-front set out for Freetown to complain about the lamentable conditions they were facing while fighting the rebels from Liberia. They had not been paid for three or four months and lacked even the basic necessities of food. It was a lightning move that completely surprised everyone. It may even have been a spontaneous action rather than a planned maneuver, but whatever it was, the demonstration of displeasure was so successful that at some point it became evident that with just a little more force the soldiers could completely overthrow the government.

They came with automatic weapons, rocket launchers, machine guns, and mounted, large-caliber cannons. The State House was one of the first targets, next the armory, and from there they captured the various radio stations and other targets of opportunity. Somehow the president, the vice president, and certain other leaders of the political party in power were not taken during this initial strike.

The fighting broke out on their arrival in Freetown that morning. Although people who were not part of the government were not targets, they were, nevertheless, in great danger. Panic broke out as people raced for safety. People carrying loads dropped them to run. Vehicle drivers trying to flee took excessive chances at excessive speed, and many accidents took place.

Word of the strike spread rapidly to the outlying areas of the city, causing all stores, shops, and kiosks to close immediately. All buses and taxis disappeared, and since there was no public transportation people had to walk or run long distances to get back to their homes. Others quickly went to the schools to get their children.

Finally, during the afternoon, Captain Strasser, one of the leaders of the uprising, came on the radio and announced that the government had been overthrown.

For the most part, people seemed happy about the coup d'etat. Yet some uncertainty existed because the leaders of the previous government had not been detained or arrested. Moreover, the BBC broadcast a report supposedly from President Momoh that he and his troops had put down a mutiny among the army troops. For some time we were uncertain as to who was really in control of things.

Reports trickled in that President Momoh was in hiding, that the Guinean troops were protecting him, that a large force of troops from Guinea were en route to rescue him, that he had taken refuge in the U.S. Embassy or the U.S. Consulate, or that he had escaped and was presently in Conakry, Guinea. We did not know where he was, and the coup leaders acknowledged that they did not know where he was.

Military discipline broke down in many cases, with soldiers demanding money, food, gasoline, and other amenities from civilians. Worst of all, some began to go from house to house in the better neighborhoods to confiscate cars and vans. Unfortunately, many of those who commandeered these vehicles did not know how to drive, had never driven in their life, and had not the least idea of how to go about it. Some drove away in first gear and never shifted again until finally the transmission seized up. Others were driven until the gasoline was gone, and then they were abandoned to be stripped by thieves. Cars were used as trucks to carry off loot—new cars with heavy loads on the roof—and interiors were destroyed through such use. The new drivers turned the cars over, crashed them, ran into the bush, burned them, sold them. The problem was so serious that twenty soldiers died of car accidents, and many more were seriously injured.

Soldiers came to our home on the first day of the coup and demanded that we open our gate. They were going to take our vehicle. Our neighbors, about fifteen of them, came to our defense, telling the soldiers that we were missionaries and that they should leave us alone.

Thank God, they did leave us alone, but they took four cars from some other neighbors. Later we were told that this very group of soldiers had a serious accident with one of the cars they had taken. After they left us I made a sign saying "MISSIONARY COMPOUND" and wired it to our front gate. It seemed to help, for no one else came after our car.

All the dogs of the neighborhood ran back and forth like demented creatures frantic with fear. Our own dog, Pierre, literally trembled. The constant gunfire was unsettling to say the least. All through the night we could hear the gunfire. We lay in our bed wondering, Will we hear a vehicle full of soldiers drive to our gate and in loud, demanding voices order that they be let in? Will they require us to open our home and, at gunpoint, demand money or our car? Will they loot our entire home, abuse us, threaten us, hurt us?

We lay there in the dark praying. There was no electricity. We had a guard, but he was scared to death. Looters were running amok, military discipline was gone, drunken soldiers used the situation to enrich themselves and to abuse others, and bullets were flying freely. Yet our Father knew we were there, and He loved us with a special love. He would not let anything happen to us without working all things together in His will. Finally, we went to sleep.

With the new morning, the shooting and looting continued. The carnival of chaos continued. The opportunity for the desperately poor to gain possessions that would be unimaginable in the normal course of their lives continued. They knew it was wrong, that it was a shame to them and their country, but the truly poor did not quibble over a rationale to take from the rich. To them their poverty was sufficient justification. So the looting continued.

After several days, the coup leader, Captain Strasser, declared over the radio that the National Provisional Ruling Council, as it called itself, decreed that all people who had had their cars commandeered could come and reclaim them. A great many of the cars had been badly abused and suffered damage through accidents and misuse. Of course, many such vehicles were never recovered. And, unfortunately, none of these losses were covered by insurance inasmuch as the damage was due to an insurrection.

When the soldiers broke into the homes of the leaders of the previous government, they took what they wanted in carloads and then told civilians to come and get what they wanted. This turned loose a looting frenzy that was startling. The word spread like wildfire that permission had been granted for the looting of certain houses. The looters came by thousands and carried away loads on their head either to their home or to some location where they would store their booty while they ran back to get more. Everything was stolen—furniture, money, clothes, plumbing, doors, windows, light fixtures, carpets, pots, pans, dishes, appliances, the roof, everything. Even cars that had been disabled to keep them from being driven away were dismantled. The looting continued for several days.

In some cases groups of toughs would steal the booty from the looters as they left the houses being looted. Fights broke out with people arguing over the right of ownership of an item both parties were trying to steal. It was a madhouse with thousands struggling and fighting to get to the booty, steal it, and somehow get it out of the house and safely to their own home.

And yet, for many it seemed to have the atmosphere of a carnival. People were laughing and shouting and encouraging each other when they were not fighting

with each other. The soldiers, at this time, were not trying to stop the looting, but they occasionally tried to
regain a degree of order by shooting their guns, and hundreds of the looters would take off running for cover. But
they were laughing. It was like a game of tag. As soon as
the soldiers stopped chasing them, they turned and went
back to the chaos and looting. The soldiers were not
actually trying to shoot anybody at this time. They
would shoot into the air and people seemed to realize
that they were in no danger unless they pushed the soldiers too far by a direct challenge to their authority.

The fighting continued on throughout the following
day and the next night. The gunfire was constant. Some
of it was from afar off, but too much of it was immediately surrounding our home. From the windows of our
home we could see soldiers running up and down the
roads and paths shooting at people. From our front door
we could observe the mayhem continuing unabated.

Finally, on the third day of the coup, the military
sent soldiers to stop the looting, but the looting frenzy
was not as easy to stop as it had been to start. Looters
went in dozens of directions, and the soldiers could not
cover all the avenues and pathways that the looters
took. The gunfire that we had heard for days now came
to the very walls of our compound. Looters trying to
run with their loads were chased. Unfortunately for us,
many of the looters were our neighbors. The teenage
son of one of our neighbors was bayoneted a couple of
times, but not seriously wounded. Some were shot and
killed, and others were wounded. Brazenly, some resist-
ed giving up the items they had stolen. After a couple of
hours of shooting and chasing looters, most of the looting stopped.

Many, many people died. Some of them died in opposition to the coup, but most of them were looters killed

by soldiers. The numbers were never reported on the radio, but here and there the stories filtered out: seventeen killed looting the Nissan garage, twelve killed looting the government rice warehouse, twenty killed in car accidents, two killed at State House, an untold number killed on the east side of town, five here, fifteen there, and on and on.

All members of the previous political party that ruled the country and some senior military officers were put into the government prison at Pademba Road in Freetown.

As more time passed the status of the coup became more and more clear. Captain Valentine Strasser was named as the chairman of the twenty-man National Provisional Ruling Council. He had been the spokesman on the radio since the beginning of the takeover. He was a young man about twenty-seven years old. His second in command was Lieutenant Musa, who was only twenty-one years old. The council took steps to reassure the International Monetary Fund, the World Bank, diplomats, and various world bodies that they would continue to honor all of Sierra Leone's commitments, that this was a "bloodless" coup that was popular with the people, that all foreigners would be safe, that it was strictly an internal problem. They also apologized for any inconveniences caused.

After several days, Captain Strasser broadcast an appeal for all businesses, government offices, and educational institutions to reopen for normal operation. He also instituted a 6:00 P.M. to 6:00 A.M. curfew and stated that violators would be shot on sight. Looters and vandals would be shot on sight as well. Although these moves helped quiet the situation, looting continued and the commandeering of vehicles continued. Consequently, business did not return to normal for some days. People needed to regain confidence that they and their property would be secure.

Nine of our pastors at various times made the effort to come to our home to check on us and to make sure we were all right. Two of them who were also soldiers came and spent the night sleeping in our yard in order to guard us. These men walked long distances through dangerous situations to reach us and then had to walk back.

Inasmuch as there was a curfew in force, we were unable to return to business as usual. We could not have night church services, and we could not operate our Bible college. Because there was no public transportation, because businesses were afraid to reopen, to sell or deliver products, because private transportation would not go on the road, and because workmen could not go to their jobs, our construction work was at a standstill.

On Saturday, May 2, 1992, one of our pastors came to us and asked if we were going to leave Sierra Leone. He had heard that American citizens were going to be evacuated. We were quite surprised at this statement and tended to reject it as just another of the many rumors that were floating around. Nevertheless, I went to a neighbor's house to call the U.S. Embassy. I was shocked to hear that there was a planned evacuation and that I should report to the Mama Yoko Hotel, where government agents would explain in detail all arrangements.

We had not been anywhere since the fighting had started; we were lying low and doing our best to keep ourselves and our vehicle out of sight. How were we to get to the Mama Yoko Hotel? We had no choice but to take a chance and see if we could get through.

Amazingly, the trip there was quite uneventful. We passed through a couple of military checkpoints, but we were not harassed and reached the hotel without incident. Inside the hotel in a large meeting room, many

Americans were gathered listening to instructions and filling out forms to get on the special flights that had been chartered for this evacuation. U.S. government agents said they had received intelligence indicating that the situation could deteriorate and in their judgment we should evacuate immediately. There were to be two flights, one the next morning at 8:00 A.M. and the other at 8:00 A.M. on Monday morning, May 4, 1992.

My first reaction was to reject all of this and see things through, but the agents gave me second thoughts. These agents are well educated and especially trained to analyze all the factors that exist to forecast future developments. I could not help but wonder if it would not be foolish to ignore the warning being given. After all, the U.S. State Department was ordering all dependents of the U.S. diplomatic corp to evacuate immediately. Most of the men would also be going, leaving only a skeleton crew to operate the embassy. All around the meeting room, Americans were busy filling out the evacuation forms.

It was impossible for me to evacuate by the next morning. There was just too much to do before I could go. It was Saturday afternoon, all businesses were closed and would remain so at least until Monday, and they might not even open then. The 6:00 P.M. curfew prevented us from leaving our house in the evening to make any of the arrangements. We had fifteen hours to get ready for the first evacuation flight.

We had three options: Abbie and I could both go, she could go and I stay, or we could both stay. When I presented the options to Abbie, she quickly reduced the three options to two: if I did not go, she was not going to go. That was emphatic. We began to consider the alternatives and what would be involved with each choice. If we both went, we would have to put our dog to sleep, no small matter inasmuch as he had been like a family

member. We would have to arrange means of transportation to get to the evacuation, set up meetings with the
National Board for the ongoing operation of the churches and the Bible college, make various arrangements relative to construction projects, get rid of perishable food,
arrange for the protection of our home and property, and
pack all important items in the single carry-on bag that
each of us would be allowed. Dozens of things had to be
done. It was obvious that we could not evacuate in time
for the first flight on Sunday morning. We then began to
consider the Monday morning flight. Even that flight
seemed doubtful, possible but doubtful. Too many people would have to be contacted, and under the circumstances our ability to contact people was extremely
questionable.

We prayed for guidance from God, and in the end we
felt we should stay and have confidence that the Lord
would keep us and protect us. Our pastors sincerely
appreciated our decision. They loved us and did not want
us to go. And our love for them and the work would not
allow us to leave if things were not properly arranged for
the continuity of the churches.

When the evacuation flight left on Monday morning
we knew we had burned a bridge behind us, but we felt
good about our decision. In the days following we kept
our eyes and ears open, alert to signs of the prophesied
deterioration, but strangely, each passing day seemed to
belie the embassy forecast. Military discipline seemed to
improve steadily. Rogue soldiers were beaten and
thrown into prison.

Tentatively, people began to stick their heads out of
their hiding places to see if it was safe to come out.
Some of the businesses opened their doors, and some of
the taxis came out of hiding. Most of the looting
stopped. No more cars were commandeered. A huge

demonstration at the National Sports Stadium involving all school children expressed support for the new government. Schools reopened. The curfew was pushed back to 10:00 P.M. and then further back to 12:00 midnight. Our churches were able to have their night services; our Bible college was able to begin classes again. Gunfire was heard only at infrequent intervals.

Only God knows what tomorrow holds. We had just received one more lesson from Him in the art of trusting His leadership.

During all of this, one of our church buildings was destroyed and the new government notified another of our churches that it would be displaced, but none of our people were injured and none of them were killed.

THIRTY-ONE

EVEN THOUGH THERE had been a coup d'etat, war continued against the rebels. They were not satisfied with a new government; they wanted to be the new government. As the war continued, it grew increasingly ugly and considerably more complicated.

It started with a group of dissidents near the border with Liberia. They had been armed and sponsored by warring elements that were endeavoring to overthrow the Liberian government.

The Sierra Leonean army fought the rebel faction, but some elements of the army had become resentful of what they perceived as neglect of their needs while fighting the enemy. Consequently, that element had overthrown the Sierra Leonean government and established military rule. The rebels refused to join or cooperate with the new regime, so the war continued.

To further complicate matters, a large portion of the army was perturbed about the coup. They were happy that the previous government had been ousted, but they felt the new leaders were too young, inexperienced, unqualified, and low in rank to become their bosses. They believed that the quirk of fate or a moment of luck that caused the coup to succeed did not mean the coup leaders should become heads of state. Instead, other more popular and more senior military leaders should have that honor.

Of course, the coup leaders felt otherwise and promptly arrested the most popular military leader in the country, sent him to prison, and later had him executed along with other supposed enemies. This, of course, further alienated the army from the new military leaders.

Inside Freetown, military discipline was fairly well maintained, but in the interior it began to deteriorate badly, with large segments deserting to form marauding groups of bandits. Many of the soldiers and officers who did not desert stayed within the army but operated as inside agents to supply information to the rebels or to the newly formed bandit groups.

The new military bandit groups not only rebelled against the new government, but they were equally, if not more so, motivated by a lust for power and wealth. These deserters, who consisted of several unconnected groups under different leadership, raided towns and villages all over the country. They were unbelievably cruel and vicious as they left a trail of blood, death, burnt homes, rape, and destruction everywhere they went. Their targets were always unarmed innocent civilians, and their objective was always loot and power. Mutilations, decapitations, disembowelings, and death by being burned alive were common acts perpetrated by both rebels and deserters to create terror. Thousands were arbitrarily shot to death for little or no provocation, but many were killed because they had seen the faces of the deserters and could identify them. This reign of terror caused 1,500,000 to 2,000,000 people to flee their homes to find safety wherever they could as refugees.

Vast camps were set up to shelter and feed these displaced people. The country did the best it could, but these camps were, nevertheless, nothing more than squalid tent cities, ghettos without water or electricity, inadequate in every regard.

Many of the refugees went to the main cities, causing great over-crowding. Bo Town swelled from a population of 50,000 to nearly 600,000 almost overnight. People who were fortunate to have a roof over their head were sleeping twenty-five to thirty to a room on the floors. Many had no roof over them, no shelter, so they slept on the streets or sidewalks.

The rebels and deserters effectively isolated the interior cities by attacking any vehicles that dared to go upon the roads leading there. These isolated cities, filled with refugees, were thus cut off from receiving basic supplies. Food supplies dwindled until the world community took notice and got involved. By then, the situation had become desperate. People were dying from starvation and disease at a rapid rate. They were so weakened by a lack of food that they had no ability to withstand any sickness, so as diseases spread through their crowded quarters, they died within days of the first symptoms.

Efforts were made to carry food to them by military convoys, but the failure rate was so great that the convoys were discontinued. An airlift was also tried, but this effort was inadequate, because the runways were too short and the airplanes too small to carry sufficient supplies. They were only able to meet the minimum nutritional needs of two thousand children when there were hundreds of thousands of needy children. Of course, there were hundreds of thousands of adults, also, but the airlift had focused on trying to save the children.

In the region of Bo Town and Kenema over one million people were starving. Foreign experts working with international relief organizations, like the Red Cross, evaluated the situation and reported that the logistics were such that it would take two years to correct. Yet these people could not wait two years. In two years, tens of thousands would die from starvation and disease. Over one hundred thousand could die in that two years.

In that part of the country we had nineteen churches closed by the war. The villages were deserted. The pastors, with their families, had to flee into the bush, often hiding there for weeks without food.

The rivers and streams were polluted with bloated bodies bringing the inevitable epidemic of cholera. Many of our people contracted cholera, but, thank God, I know of none who died from it.

We did not have the means to provide food for the general public, so we tried to do the best we could by flying in aid for our own people. They greatly appreciated the aid, but it was inadequate in the face of the need.

Many of our pastors, their families, and their saints slept on bare floors or the ground for months. I saw their bodies waste away from insufficient food. Yet I was encouraged and inspired by the spirit they manifested through these hardships.

In the very midst of this tragedy called Sierra Leone, God brought forth revival out of despair and glory out of destruction and death. The war turned people's mind to God as never before. In Freetown we now had twenty-three churches with a constituency near five thousand. Several of the churches conducted double sessions to accommodate the crowds. Nationwide, we had eighty-seven hundred people in 1995.

Many of the displaced pastors preached wherever they could. These were men who had walked out of a hell of men's making, and when they stood in the pulpit to preach they did it with power and anointing. In all of our churches that were in operation we experienced growth and revival.

Many of our displaced pastors repeatedly put their

lives on the line by going back into rebel-controlled territory to check on their churches and to see what had become of their members. All of them had barely escaped with their lives when first driven out, and a number of them had narrow escapes the second and third times when reentering their villages. They literally risked their lives trying to reopen their churches.

Pastor James Sesay could not sit within the relative safety of Freetown while his church remained in the war region. At considerable risk he went back and at service time he sounded the church bell. Rebels or no rebels, he intended to have church if any people were left in the area to which he could minister. Here and there, people who had been in hiding came out of the bush, tremendously happy to hear the sound of the church bell again. The church represented hope and encouragement to these whose lives had lost all sense of normalcy. That pastor's courage and faith will not be forgotten by the people of the region, nor will it be forgotten by God in the judgment of rewards.

Brother Jonathan Moses Kondoba, one of the refugee pastors, had escaped with his family by the very narrowest of margins. He would have been dead if a rebel's gun had not jammed. They hid for many days in the bush, then over many miles made their way to a refugee camp near Freetown. They had nothing. They had lost all they owned.

Brother Kondoba spent no time wallowing in self-pity. Instead, he began to preach in the camp. At first, just a few gathered in one of the tent shelters, but the crowd continued to grow until two large tents were filled to overflowing. Hundreds packed in. It was standing room only. And they were not bashful about praying. They repented, were baptized, and received the Holy Ghost.

God can take the devil's most terrible atrocities and use them to magnify His own great name. I believe that Christ, in His mercy, has used this national tragedy to turn the people of Sierra Leone toward salvation. All our ministers, even those who suffered most, saw the hand of God in all that happened. The horror of the war opened the door for revival as never before.

As of 1995, the war was in its fourth year. In that same four years about five thousand souls had experienced their personal Pentecost.

THIRTY-TWO

By THE BEGINNING of 1996 we had fifty-four congregations operating, and the work was experiencing widespread growth. Although we first came to Sierra Leone in late 1975, and although a good number received the Holy Ghost in 1976 and 1977, the revival really began in 1978. From that time onward our altars have always been full. From the middle of 1978 until the end of 1995, it was a rare occurrence to have an evangelistic service where nobody received the Holy Ghost. In fact, I could count on my fingers the number of evangelistic services we were in when nobody received the Holy Ghost. The result was so constant that it was expected; the only question was how many would receive.

From mid 1978 through the end of 1995 we averaged 2.7 people receiving the Holy Ghost every day. From the time of our arrival in Africa through the end of 1995 the average was 2.5 people receiving the Holy Ghost every day for over twenty years.

The excitement of constant revival can never be forgotten. The ready response of simple people to the gospel never ceased to amaze us. When the people heard the Word of God they just believed it and reacted in obedience.

Altars filled and seekers repented, gave thanks, praised God, and spoke in tongues as the Spirit gave them utterance. It was a real move of God. They did not speak in tongues as people gave them the utterance, but as God gave them the utterance. We endeavored to be certain that every experience was real. Systems were established to record all evangelistic results. That system was then cross-checked by yet another recording system to verify the accuracy of all numbers.

There were many services where only a few would receive the Holy Ghost, but it was also common to be in services where ten, fifteen, twenty, twenty-five, or thirty or more would receive the Holy Ghost. I am not referring to special conferences, but just within the regular services of local churches.

Visitors from America were always thrilled when preaching there. They could expect their ministry to produce at least forty new births each week and possibly much more. Many left with a burden to see such results in America, a renewed appreciation for the simplicity of faith, and a determination to see that same kind of faith in operation within their pastorate back in America.

A teenaged son of one of our fine California pastors came to visit us in Sierra Leone. Although he professed no call to preach, we nevertheless used him to speak in some of our churches. He had never preached before and his inexperience was obvious. Yet this sincere young man tried to minister, and, glory to God, fifty-three people received the Holy Ghost. When he returned to his family in California, he went with something that he did not have or acknowledge when he came to Africa, namely, a call to preach the gospel.

Revival continued in every church through every week and every month. Open-air services were common where many received the Holy Ghost. Miracles of healing took place in these services—the lame walked, the deaf heard, the blind saw, Muslims converted from Islam to Christianity, and worship was enthusiastic, spiritual, and uninhibited. The preaching was apostolic and anointed. God honored His Word just as He promised He would and gave His Holy Spirit to those who believed.

None of our churches contained a baptistery, but nobody ever complained about having to walk a few miles to be baptized in Jesus' name. Rarely was there a baptismal service with only one person to be immersed. Usually, there were five to thirty-five candidates for baptism. After experiencing services with multiple baptisms one gets the feeling that this is the way it is supposed to be, that this is the way it happened in the Acts of the Apostles.

In a three-week period in late 1995 a mighty deluge from heaven inundated our churches. In that brief period over three hundred were baptized into Jesus Christ. They were baptized in water and in His Spirit.

This wonderful outpouring did not happen by accident. Rather, it happened because people of God agreed together to make it happen. They intensified their outreach, went into the streets, preached in the markets, at bus stops, on street corners, in open fields, and anywhere a crowd could gather. The entirety of the church membership was motivated and activated. It was an organized apostolic attack, a motivated military maneuver, an effervescent evangelistic effort, an awesome outreach for the unreached, a spiritual spearhead to save souls, and it met with the same manifestations displayed on the Day of Pentecost in Acts 2.

The stories of great revival are so many that some of the accounts flow together in our memory. In later years it seems like one long revival, and maybe that is the truest picture of what happened. Yet that revival took place in many towns and villages, in many tribal languages, at different times, and by the dedication of many different evangelists.

Numbers and statistics can be dead and dry; they

cannot convey the power in an individual service or the glory that a person feels when hearing the cry of new-born spiritual babies. To some degree, however, they reveal that Sierra Leone has truly experienced a latter-rain outpouring of God's Spirit.

STATISTICS AS OF DECEMBER 1995

- Average of 2.5 people receiving the Holy Ghost and water baptism every day for over twenty years.
- 54 churches and preaching points, an average of 2.7 started per year
- 18,000 received the Holy Ghost
- 17,400 received water baptism in the name of Jesus Christ
- 8,500 constituents
- 81 ministers (19 were public schoolteachers and 3 were school principals)
- 9 military chaplains
- 9 Bible college instructors
- 9 National Board members
- 6 national Ladies Auxiliary Board members
- 3 national Youth Board members
- 1 national director of music
- 27 pieces of property (real estate)
- 20 structures (church buildings)
- 4 national offices
- 1 headquarters church with a 1,000-seat capacity
- 2 Bible college classrooms
- 1 Bible college chapel
- 1 Bible college conducting a three-year course resulting in diploma and granting a Bachelor of Sacred Theology degree after eight years of study
- Finally, the United Pentecostal Church of Sierra Leone has been nationalized. The church is self-governing and self-propagating.

To God be the glory! He and only He, is the fountain of all spiritual benefit. He bought, brought, and sustained revival. He raised up the evangelists, pastors, and teachers who served as the vessels of revival. His Word was the foundation upon which He built, and His Spirit was the life force within the church. That He allowed me to be even a small part of what He has done in Sierra Leone has been the highest honor of my life.

The church in Sierra Leone is His. It belongs to Him. He is both the founder and the foundation.

I love Him, but what is much more important and wonderful is that He loves me and has chosen me to be His! To know Him is everything, and to be known of Him is inexpressible glory. To be used of God is the greatest privilege in life. We each owe Him an infinite, unpayable debt. He has given so much, forgiven so much, and loved so much that the heart's cry of the born-again Christian must be for the privilege to give in return to Him, to love Him, to serve Him. I thank God that I have been allowed that privilege.

THIRTY-THREE

GOD HAS BEEN GOOD to us over the years. In 1996, we were in our twenty-second year as foreign missionaries. Over eighteen thousand had received the Holy Ghost and over seventeen thousand had been baptized in Jesus' name. We had fifty-four churches and preaching points. Our Bible college continued to train prospective ministers for future growth.

The quality of our Sierra Leonean leaders was ever improving, and as it did, I realized more and more that I was needed less and less. I had already delegated many of the duties of leadership to national leaders, and although I was still the national superintendent, my function had become that of an advisor and an administrator. With much training and with numerical and spiritual growth, the men on our National Board had developed into capable leaders. Leadership had gradually shifted from the foreign missionaries to the Sierra Leoneans.

It was as it should be. The children had grown, matured, and become adults. I was feeling somewhat like a grandfather watching my grandchildren play in the yard and seeing their parents, my children, supervising them. I was pleased at the picture and yet strangely melancholy. I was proud of my children, if such is the proper word, but aware that a new generation had come on the scene and that I had to move on to make room for them. I had run my leg of the race. Now it was time to pass the baton to new leaders.

From the beginning it had been our goal to develop an indigenous church, to work ourselves out of a job. Our work was done. I was not needed. They could carry on without me.

The roll call of Sierra Leone's mighty men is long and inspiring. It is blood washed and Spirit filled. It is a list of people who stand tall in the eyes of God and who will lead the church forward and upward until the coming of Messiah Jesus.

Even as I loved them, so did they love Sister O'Keefe and me. To other people I was just Brother O'Keefe, but to them I was an apostle of God, because I had brought them the apostolic gospel. I had founded the church, but now I had to decrease. Yet as I decreased they loved me and revered me the more.

It was time—time to leave, to commit them into the hands of our faithful God. It was time for the tears of departure.

As a fifteen-year-old boy I was walking through Nichol Park in Richmond, California. It was a large park, and walking through it could take some time. It was Saturday afternoon, and a friend and I were on our way home from town.

The previous evening, and all morning, my mind had been totally engrossed with the thoughts of God.

Suddenly, while standing upright with my eyes wide open, I saw a vision. I saw multitudes of black faces weeping and praising God with uplifted hands. Their expressions reflected a love for Jesus Christ that transcended common emotion. Written in each line of their faces was an inexpressible gratitude for Calvary.

Then the Spirit of God spoke to me: "Will you give

Me your life that this might happen? Will you surrender to Me so that these might know Me? Will you let Me use you to create the beauty that I have shown you?"

The vision faded away and left me stunned. I had never had a vision before. I was just a boy, but I knew that more than anything in the world, I wanted that vision fulfilled in my life.

The new Sierra Leone National Headquarters facility was completed and dedicated. Over seven hundred people stood in the beautiful new church with hands of surrender lifted to God. They shouted and sang. They danced in the aisles and talked in tongues. They wept for joy. They prayed. They praised the name of the Lord Jesus Christ, and the glory of God filled the temple.

Mission accomplished. Vision fulfilled.